5-INGREDIENT MEDITERRANEAN COOKBOOK

130 Quick, Easy, and Healthy Recipes for Breakfast, Lunch, Snacks, Dinner, Side Dishes, Desserts, and Drinks – Perfect for Busy Families

TABLE of CONTENTS

Introduction.. 5

The Mediterranean Diet: Simple, Healthy, and Delicious.. 6

The Powerful Health Benefits of the Mediterranean Diet.. 6

The Mediterranean Diet's Flexibility...................... 6

Why 5 Ingredients?... 7

How to Maximize Flavor with Minimal Ingredients.. 7

The Magic of Mediterranean Seasoning................ 7

Tips for Using Fresh and Pantry Ingredients........ 7

Essential Mediterranean Pantry Staples................ 7

Meal Prep the Mediterranean Way...................... 7

Budget-Friendly Ingredients............................... 8

The Benefits of Seasonal Eating.......................... 8

Minimal Equipment Required............................. 8

Enjoy the Brand-New Diet and Lifestyle.............. 8

Chapter 1
Breakfast.. 9

Honey and Almond Oatmeal.............................. 10

Spinach and Cheese Egg Muffins........................ 10

Simple Shakshuka.. 11

Quinoa Breakfast Bowl with Tomatoes................ 11

Mediterranean Omelette.................................... 12

Creamy Avocado Smoothie................................ 12

Mediterranean Spinach and Feta Quesadilla......... 13

Eggplant and Tomato Bake................................ 13

Za'atar and Olive Oil Bread............................... 14

Mediterranean Fruit Bowl................................. 14

Mediterranean Smoothie................................... 15

Bruschetta with Mozzarella, Tomato, and Pesto..... 15

Spinach and Feta Scrambled Eggs....................... 16

Baked Zucchini Frittata.................................... 16

Greek Yogurt with Honey and Nuts.................... 17

Avocado Toast with Olive Oil............................ 17

Çılbır (Turkish Poached Eggs with Yogurt).......... 18

Mediterranean Breakfast Wrap........................... 18

Tortilla de Patatas (Spanish Potato Omelette)....... 19

Ricotta and Fig Toast....................................... 19

Chapter 2
Lunch.. 20

Mediterranean Tuna Salad................................. 21

Roasted Beet Salad with Walnuts........................ 21

Baked Lemon Herb Salmon............................... 22

Greek Chickpea Salad....................................... 22

Stuffed Bell Peppers.. 23

Lentil Soup... 23

Mediterranean Stuffed Avocados........................ 24

Caprese Salad... 24

Garlic Lemon Shrimp Skewers........................... 25

Avgolemono (Greek Lemon Chicken Soup).......... 25

Piyaz (Turkish White Bean Salad)....................... 26

Hummus and Pomegranate Bulgur Bowl.............. 26

Herbed Turkey Meatballs.................................. 27

Zucchini Soup.. 27

Greek Salad... 28

Spicy Shrimp and Avocado Salad....................... 28

Grilled Chicken with Tzatziki Sauce.................... 29

Spinach and Cheese Stuffed Mushrooms.............. 29

Zucchini Noodles with Pesto............................. 30

Roasted Bell Pepper and Mozzarella Panini.......... 30

Chapter 3
Snacks.. 31

Zucchini Fritters... 32

Tahini Sauce.. 32

Roasted Chickpeas... 33

Roasted Red Pepper Dip................................... 33

Watermelon and Feta Salat................................ 34

Mediterranean Deviled Eggs.............................. 34

Herbed Goat Cheese with Crackers..................... 35

Labneh (Thickened Yogurt)............................... 35

Greek Tzatziki Dip.. 36

Hummus with Olive Oil and Paprika................... 36

Simple Pesto.. 37

Spiced Nuts (Marcona Almonds)........................ 37

Baba Ganoush.. 38

Garlic and Herb Labneh Balls............................ 38

Marinated Olives... 39

Baked Pita Chips wit Hummus........................... 39

Stuffed Mini Bell Peppers..........................40
Grilled Halloumi Cheese with Lemon.......................40
Kolokithakia Tiganita (Fried Zucchini)..................41
Spanakopita Bites (Mini Spinach and Feta Pies)......41
Dolmas (Stuffed Grape Leaves)..................42
Mezze Platter..................43

Chapter 4
Dinner..........................44
Lemon Garlic Shrimp Pasta..................45
Tomato Basil Risotto..................45
Mediterranean Chicken Skewers..................46
Herbed Salmon with Spinach..................46
Baked Cod with Tomatoes..................47
Garlic Butter Scallops..................47
Grilled Swordfish..................48
Lahanodolmades (Stuffed Cabbage Rolls)..................48
Garlic and Herb Baked Cod..................49
Mediterranean Eggplant Bake..................49
Spinach and Feta Stuffed Chicken..................50
Rosemary Lamb Chops..................50
Garlic Butter Shrimp with Asparagus..................51
Calamari with Lemon and Garlic..................51
Greek-Style Pork Tenderloin..................52
Lemon Herb Tilapia..................52
Keftedes (Greek Meatballs)..................53
Lemon Garlic Turkey..................53
Mediterranean Tuna Steak..................54
Mediterranean Beef Stir-Fry..................54
Lemon and Caper Chicken Piccata..................55
Kofta Kebab..................55
Sweet Potatoes with Hummus and Chickpeas..................56
Mussels in White Sauce..................56

Chapter 5
Side Dishes..................57
Honey and Thyme Roasted Vegetables..................58
Lemon Garlic Quinoa..................58
Garlic Roasted Potatoes withOregano..................59
Simple Greek Rice Pilaf..................59
Grilled Asparagus with Lemon..................60
Broccoli with Lemon and Garlic..................60
Grilled Zucchini..................61
Garlic Roasted Cauliflower..................61
Cucumber Feta Salad..................62
Arugula and Parmesan Salad..................62
Turkish Green Beans with Almonds..................63

Spanakorizo (Spinach Rice)..................63
Farro with Mushrooms and Carrots..................64
Caramelized Onions and Peppers..................64

Chapter 6
Desserts..................65
Lemon Olive Oil Cake..................66
Honey Ricotta with Fresh Berries..................66
Honey Almond Cookies..................67
Fig and Honey Tart..................67
Chocolate-Dipped Apricots..................68
Lemon Ricotta Cheesecake..................68
Honey and Cinnamon Baked Grapefruit..................69
Pomegranate and Nuts Frozen Yogurt Slice..................69
Grapes in Muscat Syrup..................70
Mahalabia (Middle Eastern Milk Pudding)..................70
Yogurt and Berry Parfait..................71
Panna Cotta with Honey..................71
Pomegranate Sorbet..................72
Sesame Bars (Pasteli)..................72
Orange and Almond Cake..................73
Stuffed Dates with Nuts and Goat Cheese..................73
Baked Pears with Honey..................74
Baklava Bites..................74
Almond Nougat..................75
Rosewater Saffron Rice Pudding..................75

Chapter 7
Refreshers..................76
Lemon Mint Cooler..................77
Traditional Hot Turkish Tea with Lemon..................77
Iced Greek Frappe..................78
Pomegranate Spritzer..................78
Rosewater Lemonade..................79
Minty Yogurt Lassi..................79
Ayran (Cucumber Yogurt Drink)..................80
Fig and Honey Iced Tea..................80
Watermelon Basil Cooler..................81
Limoncello Spritz..................81

Cooking Measurements & Kitchen Conversions..................82
Gratitude..................83

INTRODUCTION

Welcome to the **"5-Ingredient Mediterranean Cookbook,"** your guide to making the Mediterranean diet simple, delicious, and accessible. This cookbook is designed to make cooking joyful, not stressful, by offering recipes that focus on fresh ingredients and fit into even the busiest lives. Whether you're new to this way of eating or a seasoned home cook, this book makes every meal easier and more enjoyable.

Inside, you'll find quick, easy recipes that highlight the vibrant flavors of the Mediterranean. From breakfast to dinner, each dish is crafted to bring you great taste and balanced nutrition with just five ingredients, making healthy eating effortless. With minimal prep and easy-to-follow instructions, you'll spend less time in the kitchen and more time savoring your food.

The beauty of the Mediterranean diet lies in its flexibility. It lets you adapt recipes to your taste, use seasonal ingredients, and enjoy a mix of plant-based foods, lean meats, or seafood. This diet turns the simplest ingredients into something truly special. Plus, it's a sustainable way of eating that supports long-term health and well-being.

More than just food, the Mediterranean diet is about savoring life's simple pleasures—fresh produce, heart-healthy fats, and good company. This cookbook helps you bring these flavors into your home, making every meal a celebration of wholesome food. Whether you're cooking for yourself or sharing a meal with loved ones, you'll find that these recipes make every moment around the table special.

Let this cookbook inspire you to cook with confidence, even on your busiest days. Bring the taste of the Mediterranean into your kitchen and enjoy every bite, knowing you're nourishing your body and soul with every meal!

The Mediterranean Diet: Simple, Healthy, and Delicious

The Mediterranean diet is more than just a way of eating; it's a celebration of life itself. Rooted in the culinary traditions of countries bordering the Mediterranean Sea, this diet emphasizes whole foods, fresh ingredients, and the joy of sharing meals with loved ones. It's all about balance—where every bite is packed with nutrients, every dish bursts with flavor, and each meal feels like a moment of indulgence without the guilt. With a focus on vibrant vegetables, lean proteins, whole grains, and heart-healthy fats like olive oil and nuts, the Mediterranean diet transforms even the simplest of dishes into something extraordinary. This diet isn't about strict rules or restrictions; it's about enjoying food in its most natural and delicious form.

The Powerful Health Benefits of the Mediterranean Diet

The Mediterranean diet isn't just known for its delicious flavors—it's also celebrated for its wide range of health benefits. This way of eating supports overall well-being, from improving heart health to enhancing brain function. The following are some of the most impactful health benefits that come with adopting the Mediterranean lifestyle:

Brain Health and Cognitive Function

The Mediterranean diet is more than just good for your body; it's also a brain booster. Nutrient-rich foods like fish, nuts, olive oil, and leafy greens play a key role in supporting cognitive function and brain health. By including these ingredients in your diet, you're not just feeding your body; you're also nourishing your mind, helping to keep it sharp and focused.

Reducing Inflammation

One of the Mediterranean diet's most powerful benefits is its ability to reduce inflammation. With a focus on anti-inflammatory foods like fatty fish, olive oil, nuts, and colorful vegetables, his way of eating helps manage inflammation in the body, which is linked to numerous chronic conditions. Reducing inflammation not only boosts your overall health but also supports a stronger immune system and reduces the risk of long-term illnesses.

Supporting Balanced Blood Sugar Levels

Whole grains, legumes, healthy fats, and plenty of fiber-rich foods make the Mediterranean diet a great choice for balanced blood sugar levels. This diet's emphasis on natural, unprocessed ingredients helps keep energy levels stable and minimizes blood sugar spikes, making it ideal for those looking to manage their glucose naturally and maintain a steady flow of energy throughout the day.

Weight Management

The Mediterranean diet supports healthy weight management in a sustainable way. Instead of focusing on restrictions, it encourages the consumption of satisfying whole foods that help control hunger naturally. By enjoying balanced meals that taste great, you can achieve your health goals without feeling deprived or constantly counting calories.

Promoting Better Sleep

Good sleep is another benefit of the Mediterranean diet, thanks to its inclusion of foods like nuts, seeds, and leafy greens, which are rich in nutrients that promote relaxation and restfulness. Incorporating these foods into your evening meals can help you unwind and support a good night's sleep, improving your overall well-being.

The Mediterranean Diet's Flexibility

One of the most appealing aspects of the Mediterranean diet is its flexibility. You can easily adapt recipes to suit your taste, make the most of seasonal ingredients, and explore a variety of plant-based foods, lean proteins, or seafood. This diet encourages creativity in the kitchen, allowing you to experiment with flavors and textures, making each dish your own. This adaptability makes it easy to enjoy healthy meals that fit your lifestyle, no matter how busy or varied your days are.

Why 5 Ingredients?

The heart of this cookbook lies in its simplicity: creating delicious Mediterranean recipes with just five ingredients. This approach is designed specifically for busy families who want to eat well without spending hours in the kitchen. Limiting each recipe to five ingredients helps to keep cooking stress-free, quick, and incredibly satisfying. It's all about focusing on the quality and natural flavors of each ingredient, transforming everyday meals into something special with minimal effort. For those with packed schedules, this means you can prepare wholesome dishes that are not only nutritious but also bursting with authentic Mediterranean taste. The five-ingredient rule encourages resourcefulness in the kitchen, making it easier to stick to a healthy eating plan that fits seamlessly into your daily routine.

How to Maximize Flavor with Minimal Ingredients

When you're working with just a few ingredients, every flavor counts. The Mediterranean diet makes the most of bold, simple flavors like fresh herbs, citrus, garlic, and olive oil to elevate even the most basic dish. A sprinkle of basil, a squeeze of lemon, or a drizzle of olive oil can transform a meal from ordinary to extraordinary. This focus on maximizing flavor with minimal ingredients is what makes Mediterranean cooking so appealing and satisfying.

The Magic of Mediterranean Seasonings

One of the secrets behind the rich flavors of Mediterranean dishes lies in the seasoning. Mediterranean cuisine relies on a few key herbs and spices to bring depth and brightness to every meal. Fresh herbs like oregano, basil, rosemary, and thyme are staples, adding layers of earthy or aromatic notes. Paired with warming spices like cumin, paprika, and cinnamon, these seasonings bring Mediterranean dishes to life without overpowering the natural taste of the ingredients. Whether you're making a simple salad or a hearty stew, these seasonings allow you to create bold, vibrant dishes with minimal effort, ensuring that even the simplest recipes are full of flavor.

Tips for Using Fresh and Pantry Ingredients

Blending fresh produce with pantry staples is the key to Mediterranean cooking. Fresh herbs, tomatoes, leafy greens, and fruits bring brightness to your dishes, while pantry essentials like olive oil, grains, beans, and canned tomatoes provide a strong foundation for any meal. This combination of fresh and shelf-stable ingredients makes it easy to create delicious meals with what you have on hand, keeping your cooking flexible and convenient.

Essential Mediterranean Pantry Staples

A well-stocked pantry is your secret weapon in Mediterranean cooking. Items like olive oil, whole grains, canned beans, nuts, dried herbs, and spices are the foundation of countless dishes. Having these staples on hand means you're always ready to whip up a healthy meal, no matter what's in your fridge. These ingredients are versatile, affordable, and make cooking flavorful Mediterranean dishes a breeze.

Meal Prep the Mediterranean Way

The Mediterranean diet isn't just about quick meals; it's also perfect for meal prep. Many Mediterranean dishes, from salads to stews, can be cooked in advance and stored for several days, making them ideal for busy families. You can prepare snacks, sides, or even full meals that retain their flavor and freshness over time. This approach saves you time during the week and ensures you always have healthy, ready-to-eat meals on hand. Whether you're prepping a batch of hummus or roasting a tray of vegetables, the Mediterranean way offers a practical and delicious approach to meal planning.

Budget-Friendly Ingredients

Eating Mediterranean-style doesn't have to be expensive. The diet often relies on affordable ingredients like beans, grains, and seasonal produce that deliver big flavor without breaking the bank. This approach to cooking proves that healthy eating can be both delicious and budget-friendly.

The Benefits of Seasonal Eating

Seasonal eating is a core part of the Mediterranean diet, providing fresh, flavorful ingredients that are both affordable and nutritious. By focusing on what's in season, you can create simple, budget-friendly meals while supporting local farmers. From vibrant summer produce to hearty winter vegetables, seasonal eating ensures variety and sustainability in every dish.

Minimal Equipment Required

You don't need a high-tech kitchen to cook Mediterranean dishes. These recipes are designed to be simple and straightforward, requiring only basic tools and utensils. This means anyone can enjoy Mediterranean flavors without needing to invest in fancy gadgets, making it accessible to all home cooks.

Enjoy the Brand-New Diet and Lifestyle

Embracing the Mediterranean diet is more than a change in your eating habits—it's an invitation to a new way of living. This lifestyle encourages slowing down, savoring each meal, and finding joy in food. It's about connecting with loved ones around the table, enjoying fresh and wholesome ingredients, and creating lasting memories through the simple act of sharing a meal. The Mediterranean way of life is a beautiful blend of food, community, and well-being that goes beyond the kitchen, bringing a sense of joy and fulfillment to your everyday life. Beyond just eating well, this lifestyle promotes mindfulness and balance in all aspects of life. From the vibrant colors on your plate to the rich conversations shared over meals, the Mediterranean approach reminds us to appreciate the simple pleasures. By embracing this way of living, you're not only nourishing your body but also fostering meaningful connections with the people around you.

Chapter 1

Breakfast

Honey and Almond Oatmeal

 PREPARATION TIME: 5 MINUTES

 COOKING TIME: 10 MINUTES

SERVES: 4

Nutrition Information (Per Serving):
220 Calories / 8g Fat / 32g Carbohydrates / 6g Protein / 90mg Sodium / 10g Sugar

INGREDIENTS:

- 1 cup rolled oats
- 2 cups almond milk or milk of your choice
- 2 tablespoons honey
- 1/4 cup sliced almonds
- 1/2 teaspoon ground cinnamon (option)

DIRECTIONS:

1. In a medium saucepan, bring the milk to a boil. Stir in the oats and cook for 5-7 minutes, until tender. Mix in the honey and cinnamon. Divide into bowls and top with sliced almonds before serving.
2. This recipe offers the flexibility to use your preferred type of milk, making it a versatile and delicious breakfast option.

TIP: For added texture and flavor, try stirring in a handful of fresh berries or a spoonful of nut butter before serving.

Spinach and Cheese Egg Muffins

 PREPARATION TIME: 10 MINUTES

 COOKING TIME: 20 MINUTES

 SERVES: 4

Nutrition Information (Per Serving):
120 Calories / 8g Fat / 3g Carbohydrates / 9g Protein / 180mg Sodium / 1g Sugar

INGREDIENTS:

- 6 large eggs
- 1 cup fresh spinach, chopped
- 1/4 cup feta cheese, crumbled
- 1/4 cup cherry tomatoes, diced

* Salt and pepper, to taste

DIRECTIONS:

1. Preheat your oven to 350°F (175°C). Lightly grease a muffin tin or use silicone muffin cups.
2. In a large bowl, whisk together the eggs with a pinch of salt and pepper. Stir in the chopped spinach, diced cherry tomatoes, and crumbled feta cheese.
3. Pour the egg mixture evenly into the muffin cups, filling them about three-quarters full.
4. Place the muffin tin in the preheated oven and bake for 15-20 minutes, or until the egg muffins are set and slightly golden on top.
5. Let the muffins cool slightly before removing them from the tin. Serve warm or at room temperature.

TIP: These muffins pair perfectly with a side of tzatziki sauce for an extra burst of flavor!

Simple Shakshuka

PREPARATION TIME: 10 MINUTES

COOKING TIME: 20 MINUTES

SERVES: 4

Nutrition Information (Per Serving):
250 Calories / 14g Fat / 20g Carbohydrates / 10g Protein / 450mg Sodium / 6g Sugar

INGREDIENTS:

- 4 large eggs
- 4 medium tomatoes, diced
- 1 red bell pepper, chopped
- 3 cloves garlic, minced
- 2 tablespoons olive oil

*Salt and pepper ,to taste
*Fresh parsley for garnish (optional)

DIRECTIONS:

1. Heat olive oil in a large skillet over medium heat. Add the minced garlic and chopped bell pepper, cooking until the pepper softens, about 5 minutes.
2. Stir in the diced tomatoes and simmer for about 10 minutes, until the mixture thickens slightly. Season with salt and pepper.
3. Make four small wells in the tomato mixture and crack an egg into each well. Cover the skillet and let the eggs cook until the whites are set but the yolks are still runny, about 5 minutes.
4. Garnish with fresh parsley if desired, and serve the shakshuka hot with crusty bread or pita.

Quinoa Breakfast Bowl with Tomatoes

PREPARATION TIME: 10 MINUTES

COOKING TIME: 20 MINUTES

SERVES: 4

Nutrition Information (Per Serving):
230 Calories / 8g Fat / 30g Carbohydrates / 10g Protein / 300mg Sodium / 4g Sugar

INGREDIENTS:

- 1 cup quinoa
- 2 cups water
- 1 cup cherry tomatoes, halved
- 1/2 cup crumbled feta cheese
- 2 tablespoons olive oil

*Salt and pepper, to taste
*Fresh basil for garnish (optional)

DIRECTIONS:

1. Rinse the quinoa under cold water. In a medium saucepan, bring the quinoa and water to a boil. Reduce heat, cover, and simmer for about 15 minutes, or until the water is absorbed and the quinoa is fluffy.
2. Divide the cooked quinoa into four bowls. Top each bowl with halved cherry tomatoes and crumbled feta cheese.
3. Drizzle with olive oil and season with salt and pepper.
4. Garnish with fresh basil leaves, if desired, and serve warm.

TIP: Add a poached egg on top for extra protein and richness

Mediterranean Omelette

PREPARATION TIME: 10 MINUTES

COOKING TIME: 10 MINUTES

SERVES: 4

Nutrition Information (Per Serving):
200 Calories / 14g Fat / 6g Carbohydrates / 12g Protein / 300mg Sodium / 3g Sugar

INGREDIENTS:

- 8 large eggs
- 1/2 cup crumbled feta cheese
- 1 cup cherry tomatoes, halved
- 2 tablespoons olive oil

*Salt and pepper, to taste

*Fresh basil for garnish (optional)

DIRECTIONS:

1. In a bowl, whisk the eggs until well combined. Season with salt and pepper.
2. Heat 1 tablespoon of olive oil in a non-stick pan over medium heat.
3. Pour in half of the egg mixture and cook for 2-3 minutes until the edges start to set.
4. Sprinkle half of the feta cheese and half of the cherry tomatoes over the eggs.
5. Cook for another 2-3 minutes until the eggs are fully set.
6. Fold the omelette in half and slide it onto a plate.
7. Repeat the process with the remaining egg mixture, feta, and tomatoes.
8. Garnish with chopped fresh basil, if desired, and serve immediately.

Creamy Avocado Smoothie

PREPARATION TIME: 5 MINUTES

COOKING TIME: NONE

SERVES: 4

Nutrition Information (Per Serving):
190 Calories / 10g Fat / 24g Carbohydrates / 3g Protein / 60mg Sodium / 12g Sugar

INGREDIENTS:

- 2 ripe avocados, peeled and pitted
- 1 banana
- 2 cups spinach
- 2 cups almond milk (or any milk of your choice)
- 1 tablespoon honey (or maple syrup)

*Ice cubes (optional)

DIRECTIONS:

1. In a blender, combine the avocado, banana, spinach, milk, and honey. Add a handful of ice cubes if you prefer a chilled smoothie.
2. Blend on high speed until the mixture is creamy and smooth.
3. Pour the smoothie into glasses and serve immediately.

Mediterranean Spinach and Feta Quesadilla

✗ **PREPARATION TIME:** 5 MINUTES

✓ **COOKING TIME:** 10 MINUTES

👥 **SERVES:** 4

Nutrition Information (Per Serving):
210 Calories / 12g Fat / 18g Carbohydrates / 7g Protein / 280mg Sodium / 2g Sugar

INGREDIENTS:

- 4 round tortillas (any type of your choice)
- 1 cup fresh spinach
- 1/2 cup mushrooms, sliced
- 1/4 cup feta cheese, crumbled
- 2 tablespoons olive oil

*Salt and pepper, to test

DIRECTIONS:

1. Heat 1 tablespoon of olive oil in a skillet over medium heat. Add the sliced mushrooms and spinach, cooking until the spinach is wilted and the mushrooms are tender, about 3-4 minutes.
2. Place a tortilla on a flat surface and layer half of it with the spinach and mushroom mixture. Sprinkle crumbled feta cheese on top of the vegetables.
3. Fold the tortilla in half over the filling. Heat the remaining olive oil in the skillet and cook the quesadilla on each side for about 2-3 minutes or until golden brown and crispy.
4. Slice the quesadilla into wedges and serve warm.

Eggplant and Tomato Bake

✗ **PREPARATION TIME:** 15 MINUTES

✓ **COOKING TIME:** 30 MINUTES

👥 **SERVES:** 4

Nutrition Information (Per Serving):
200 Calories / 12g Fat / 18g Carbohydrates / 5g Protein / 220mg Sodium / 6g Sugar

INGREDIENTS:

- 1 large eggplant, sliced into rounds
- 3 large tomatoes, sliced
- 2 garlic cloves, minced
- 3 tablespoons olive oil
- 1/4 cup fresh basil leaves, chopped

*Salt and pepper, to taste

DIRECTIONS:

1. Preheat your oven to 375°F (190°C).
2. Arrange the sliced eggplant and tomatoes in an alternating pattern in a large baking dish.
3. Sprinkle the minced garlic evenly over the eggplant and tomatoes. Drizzle with olive oil and season with salt and pepper.
4. Place the dish in the preheated oven and bake for about 25-30 minutes, or until the eggplant is tender and the tomatoes are slightly caramelized.
5. Once baked, sprinkle with fresh basil.

TIP: Add a drizzle of balsamic glaze for a touch of sweetness to enhance the flavors!

Za'atar and Olive Oil Bread

PREPARATION TIME: 10 MINUTES

COOKING TIME: 15 MINUTES

SERVES: 4

Nutrition Information (Per Serving):
280 Calories / 14g Fat / 30g Carbohydrates / 6g Protein / 250mg Sodium / 2g Sugar

INGREDIENTS:

- 4 whole pita breads
- 1/4 cup olive oil
- 2 tablespoons za'atar spice blend
- Sea salt, to taste

DIRECTIONS:

1. Preheat your oven to 350°F (175°C).
2. Place the pita breads on a baking sheet.
3. In a small bowl, mix the olive oil with the za'atar spice blend.
4. Brush the za'atar mixture evenly over the pita breads.
5. Sprinkle a pinch of sea salt on top.
6. Bake in the oven for 10-15 minutes, or until the bread is crispy and golden. Serve warm

TIP: Pair this bread with hummus or another sauce of your choice for dipping, or use it as a base for a simple Mediterranean-style pizza.

Mediterranean Fruit Bowl

PREPARATION TIME: 10 MINUTES

COOKING TIME: NONE

SERVES: 4

Nutrition Information (Per Serving):
80 Calories / 0g Fat / 20g Carbohydrates / 1g Protein / 5mg Sodium / 16g Sugar

INGREDIENTS:

- 1 cup watermelon, cubed
- 1 cup cantaloupe, cubed
- 1 cup grapes, halved
- 1 cup fresh berries of your choice (strawberries, blueberries, or raspberries)
- Juice of 1 lemon or lime

DIRECTIONS:

1. In a large bowl, combine the watermelon, cantaloupe, grapes, and fresh berries.
2. Drizzle the lemon or lime juice over the fruit mixture and gently toss to coat all the pieces evenly.
3. Serve immediately or refrigerate for 15-20 minutes to allow the flavors to meld.

TIP: For a savory twist, sprinkle a little crumbled feta cheese over the fruit before serving, or add a few pomegranate seeds for extra color and flavor.

Mediterranean Smoothie

PREPARATION TIME: 5 MINUTES

COOKING TIME: NONE

SERVES: 4

Nutrition Information (Per Serving):
180 Calories / 6g Fat / 24g Carbohydrates / 8g Protein / 55mg Sodium / 18g Sugar

INGREDIENTS:

- 2 cups plain Greek yogurt
- 1 cup mixed berries (strawberries, blueberries, raspberries, blackberries)
- 1 medium banana
- 1/2 cup orange juice
- 1 tablespoon honey

*Ice cubes (optional)

DIRECTIONS:

1. In a blender, combine the plain Greek yogurt, mixed berries, banana, orange juice, and honey.
2. Blend on high speed until the mixture is smooth and creamy.
3. If you prefer a colder, thicker smoothie, add a few ice cubes and blend again until well combined.
4. Pour the smoothie into four glasses and serve immediately. Enjoy!

Bruschetta with Mozzarella, Tomato, and Pesto

PREPARATION TIME: 10 MINUTES

COOKING TIME: 5 MINUTES

SERVES: 4

Nutrition Information (Per Serving):
200 Calories / 12g Fat / 18g Carbohydrates / 8g Protein / 300mg Sodium / 2g Sugar

INGREDIENTS:

- 8 slices of crusty bread (like a baguette or ciabatta)
- 2 ripe tomatoes, diced
- 1 ball (about 8 oz) fresh mozzarella, sliced
- 1/4 cup pesto sauce (see recipe on p. 37)
- 2 tablespoons olive oil

*Salt and pepper, to test
*Fresh basil leaves for garnish (optional)

DIRECTIONS:

1. Preheat a grill pan or oven broiler. Brush both sides of the bread slices with olive oil. Grill or broil the bread for 2-3 minutes on each side until golden and crispy.
2. Spread about 1 teaspoon of pesto on each slice of toasted bread. Top with a slice of fresh mozzarella and a spoonful of diced tomatoes.
3. Sprinkle the tomatoes with a pinch of salt and pepper.
4. Garnish with fresh basil leaves if desired.
5. Serve immediately.

TIP: For extra flavor, drizzle the bruschetta with a balsamic glaze before serving.

Spinach and Feta Scrambled Eggs

PREPARATION TIME: 5 MINUTES

COOKING TIME: 5 MINUTES

SERVES: 4

Nutrition Information (Per Serving):
180 Calories / 14g Fat / 3g Carbohydrates / 10g Protein / 250mg Sodium / 1g Sugar

INGREDIENTS:

- 8 large eggs
- 2 cups fresh spinach leaves
- 8 tablespoons crumbled feta cheese
- 2 tablespoon olive oil

*Salt and pepper, to taste

DIRECTIONS:

1. In a bowl, beat the eggs with a pinch of salt and pepper.
2. Heat 1 tablespoon of olive oil in a pan over medium heat. Add the spinach and cook until wilted, about 2 minutes.
3. Pour the remaining olive oil into the pan. Add the beaten eggs to the spinach. Cook, stirring gently, until the eggs are just set.
4. Sprinkle the crumbled feta over the eggs and cook for an additional minute, allowing the cheese to warm and slightly melt.
5. Serve immediately.

Baked Zucchini Frittata

PREPARATION TIME: 10 MINUTES

COOKING TIME: 25 MINUTES

SERVES: 4

Nutrition Information (Per Serving):
180 Calories / 12g Fat / 7g Carbohydrates / 10g Protein / 250mg Sodium / 2g Sugar

INGREDIENTS:

- 4 large eggs
- 2 medium zucchinis, grated
- 1/2 cup grated Parmesan cheese
- 1/4 cup chopped fresh basil
- 2 tablespoons olive oil,

*Salt and pepper, to taste

DIRECTIONS:

1. Preheat your oven to 375°F (190°C).
2. In a large bowl, beat the eggs. Mix in the grated zucchini, Parmesan, basil, salt, and pepper.
3. Heat the olive oil in an ovenproof skillet over medium heat. Pour the egg mixture into the skillet and cook for 5 minutes until the edges start to set.
4. Transfer the skillet to the oven and bake for 20 minutes, or until the frittata is set and lightly golden.
5. Let cool slightly, slice into wedges, and serve warm or at room temperature.

TIP: Pair your frittata with a light drizzle of garlic aioli or a dollop of pesto for added flavor.

Greek Yogurt with Honey and Nuts

PREPARATION TIME: 5 MINUTES

COOKING TIME: NONE

SERVES: 4

Nutrition Information (Per Serving):
220 Calories / 9g Fat / 25g Carbohydrates / 12g Protein / 65 mg Sodium / 20g Sugar

INGREDIENTS:

- 2 cups Greek yogurt
- 4 tablespoons honey
- 1/2 cup of your favorite nuts, chopped (e.g., walnuts, almonds, pistachios)

DIRECTIONS:

1. Divide Greek yogurt evenly into 4 bowls.
2. Drizzle 1 tablespoon of honey over each bowl of yogurt.
3. Sprinkle your favorite chopped nuts on top of each serving.
4. Optionally, add a pinch of cinnamon or fresh berries for extra flavor.
5. Serve immediately and enjoy!

TIP: Toast the nuts briefly in a skillet to enhance their flavor and add extra crunch to your yogurt.

Avocado Toast with Olive Oil

PREPARATION TIME: 5 MINUTES

COOKING TIME: 5 MINUTES

SERVES: 4

Nutrition Information (Per Serving):
250 Calories / 17g Fat / 22g Carbohydrates / 5g Protein / 150mg Sodium / 1g Sugar

INGREDIENTS:

- 2-3 ripe avocados
- 8 slices of whole-grain bread, or bread of your choice
- 4 tablespoons olive oil

*Salt and pepper, to taste

DIRECTIONS:

1. Toast the bread until golden brown.
2. Mash the avocados in a bowl, leaving some chunks for texture.
3. Spread the mashed avocado on each slice of toast.
4. Drizzle one tablespoon of olive oil over each slice.
5. Season with salt and pepper.
6. Serve immediately.

TIP: Top with a poached egg or sliced tomatoes for added flavor.

Çılbır (Turkish Poached Eggs with Yogurt)

PREPARATION TIME: 10 MINUTES

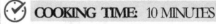
COOKING TIME: 10 MINUTES

SERVES: 4

Nutrition Information (Per Serving):
250 Calories / 18g Fat / 6g Carbohydrates / 14g Protein / 150mg Sodium / 3g Sugar

INGREDIENTS:

- 4 large eggs
- 2 cups plain Greek yogurt
- 2 tablespoons butter
- 1 teaspoon paprika
- 1 tablespoon vinegar (for poaching the eggs)

*Salt and pepper, to test
*Fresh dill or parsley, for garnish

DIRECTIONS:

1. In a small bowl, whisk the Greek yogurt with a pinch of salt and set it aside at room temperature.
2. In a medium saucepan, bring water and vinegar to a gentle simmer. Crack each egg into a small bowl, then carefully slide it into the simmering water. Poach the eggs for 3-4 minutes, until the whites are set but the yolks are still runny. Use a slotted spoon to remove the eggs and set them aside.
3. In a small pan, melt the butter over medium heat. Stir in the paprika and cook for 1 minute, or until the butter turns a deep red color.
4. Spread the seasoned yogurt on a serving plate. Place the poached eggs on top of the yogurt.
5. Drizzle the paprika-infused butter over the poached eggs and yogurt. Garnish with fresh dill or parsley, if desired, and serve immediately with crusty bread.

Mediterranean Breakfast Wrap

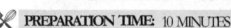
PREPARATION TIME: 10 MINUTES

COOKING TIME: 15 MINUTES

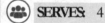
SERVES: 4

Nutrition Information (Per Serving):
280 Calories / 15g Fat / 25g Carbohydrates / 12g Protein / 500mg Sodium / 3g Sugar

INGREDIENTS:

- 4 large whole-wheat tortillas, or tortillas of your choice
- 1 cup hummus (see recipe on p. 36)
- 1 cup fresh spinach leaves
- 1/2 cup diced tomatoes
- 1/2 cup crumbled feta cheese

*Salt and pepper, to test
*Sliced black olives (optional)

DIRECTIONS:

1. Lay the tortillas flat on a clean surface.
2. Evenly spread about 1/4 cup of hummus on each tortilla.
3. Layer fresh spinach leaves, diced tomatoes, and black olives (if using) on top of the hummus.
4. Sprinkle crumbled feta cheese over the vegetables.
5. Lightly season with salt and pepper.
6. Fold the sides of the tortilla inward, then roll it up tightly from the bottom to form a wrap.
7. Serve immediately or wrap in foil for an easy, portable breakfast.

Tortilla de Patatas (Spanish Potato Omelette)

⚔ **PREPARATION TIME:** 15 MINUTES

⏱ **COOKING TIME:** 25 MINUTES

👥 **SERVES:** 4

Nutrition Information (Per Serving):
250 Calories / 14g Fat / 24g Carbohydrates / 7g Protein / 220mg Sodium / 2g Sugar

INGREDIENTS:

- 4 large eggs
- 3 medium potatoes, thinly sliced
- 1 medium onion, thinly sliced
- 1/4 cup olive oil

*Salt and pepper, to taste

DIRECTIONS:

1. Heat olive oil in a skillet over medium heat. Cook the sliced potatoes and onions, stirring occasionally, until soft (about 15 minutes). Season with salt and pepper.
2. While cooking, beat the eggs with a pinch of salt in a large bowl.
3. Transfer the cooked potatoes and onions to the eggs, stir to combine.
4. Remove excess oil from the skillet, then pour the mixture back in. Cook on low heat for 5-7 minutes until edges set.
5. Flip the omelette onto a plate, slide it back into the skillet, and cook for another 3-4 minutes until fully set.
6. Cool slightly, slice into wedges, and serve warm or at room temperature.

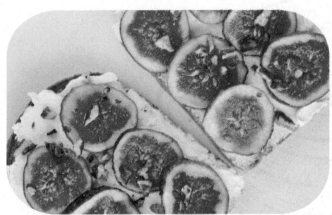

Ricotta and Fig Toast

⚔ **PREPARATION TIME:** 5 MINUTES

⏱ **COOKING TIME:** NONE

👥 **SERVES:** 4

Nutrition Information (Per Serving):
180 Calories / 6g Fat / 26g Carbohydrates / 6g Protein / 140mg Sodium / 12g Sugar

INGREDIENTS:

- 4 slices of whole grain bread (or any bread of your choice)
- 1/2 cup ricotta cheese
- 4 fresh figs, sliced
- 1 tablespoon honey
- 1/4 teaspoon cinnamon

DIRECTIONS:

1. Toast the whole grain bread slices to your desired level of crispness.
2. Evenly spread a layer of ricotta cheese on each slice of toasted bread.
3. Place the sliced figs neatly on top of the ricotta cheese.
4. Lightly drizzle honey over the figs for a touch of natural sweetness.
5. Finish by sprinkling a dash of cinnamon over the top of each toast.
6. Serve immediately as a fresh and delicious breakfast or snack.

TIP: For a touch of extra flavor, try adding a few crushed nuts like pistachios or walnuts on top for added crunch and texture!

Chapter (2)

Lunch

Mediterranean Tuna Salad

 PREPARATION TIME: 10 MINUTES

 COOKING TIME: NONE

SERVES: 4

Nutrition Information (Per Serving):
250 Calories / 15g Fat / 10g Carbohydrates / 22g Protein / 400mg Sodium / 2g Sugar

INGREDIENTS:

- 2 cans (5 oz each) tuna in water, drained
- 1 cup cherry tomatoes, halved
- 1/4 cup red onion, finely diced
- 1/4 cup Kalamata olives, halved
- 2 tablespoons olive oil

*Salt and pepper, to taste
*Fresh parsley for garnish (optional)

DIRECTIONS:

1. In a large bowl, combine the drained tuna, cherry tomatoes, red onion, and Kalamata olives.
2. Drizzle the olive oil over the salad, and toss gently to combine.
3. Season with salt and pepper to taste if needed.
4. Serve the tuna salad fresh or chill it for 30 minutes for extra flavor.

TIP: This salad pairs perfectly with some crusty bread or on a bed of greens for a light lunch!

Roasted Beet Salad with Walnuts

 PREPARATION TIME: 15 MINUTES

 COOKING TIME: 45 MINUTES (roasting time)

 SERVES: 4

Nutrition Information (Per Serving):
200 Calories / 12g Fat / 20g Carbohydrates / 4g Protein / 150mg Sodium / 10g Sugar

INGREDIENTS:

- 4 medium beets, trimmed and scrubbed
- 1/2 cup walnuts, toasted
- 4 cups mixed salad greens (arugula, spinach, etc.)
- 1/4 cup crumbled goat cheese or feta cheese (optional)

Dressing:
*2 tablespoons olive oil
*1 teaspoon honey (for added sweetness)
*Salt and pepper, to taste

DIRECTIONS:

1. Preheat the oven to 400°F (200°C). Wrap the beets in foil and roast for about 45-60 minutes, or until tender. Let them cool, then peel and slice the beets.
2. In a large bowl, combine the mixed salad greens, toasted walnuts, and crumbled goat or feta cheese.
3. In a small bowl, whisk together the olive oil, honey (if using), salt, and pepper.
4. Add the roasted beet slices to the salad. Drizzle the honey olive oil dressing over the salad and toss gently to combine.
5. Serve the salad immediately and enjoy!

Baked Lemon Herb Salmon

PREPARATION TIME: 10 MINUTES

COOKING TIME: 15-20 MINUTES

SERVES: 4

Nutrition Information (Per Serving):
250 Calories / 14g Fat / 4g Carbohydrates / 25g Protein / 150mg Sodium / 1g Sugar

INGREDIENTS:

- 4 salmon fillets (about 6 oz each)
- 2 tablespoons olive oil
- 1 lemon, thinly sliced
- 1 tablespoon fresh thyme (or 1 teaspoon dried thyme)
- 1 tablespoon fresh dill (or 1 teaspoon dried dill)

*Salt and pepper, to taste

DIRECTIONS:

1. Preheat your oven to 400°F (200°C).
2. Place the salmon fillets on a baking sheet lined with parchment paper. Drizzle olive oil over the fillets, then season with salt to taste.
3. Top each fillet with thin lemon slices, fresh thyme, and dill.
4. Bake the salmon in the preheated oven for 15-20 minutes, or until the fish is cooked through and flakes easily with a fork.
5. Serve the salmon hot with your favorite side dish or a fresh salad, if desired.

Greek Chickpea Salad

PREPARATION TIME: 10 MINUTES

COOKING TIME: NONE

SERVES: 4

Nutrition Information (Per Serving):
200 Calories / 8g Fat / 20g Carbohydrates / 7g Protein / 300mg Sodium / 4g Sugar

INGREDIENTS:

- 1 can (15 oz) chickpeas, drained and rinsed
- 1 cup cherry tomatoes, halved
- 1/2 cucumber, diced
- 1/4 cup feta cheese, crumbled
- 1/4 cup Kalamata olives

*Olive oil, for dressing (optional)
*Salt and pepper, to taste

DIRECTIONS:

1. In a large bowl, mix together the chickpeas, cherry tomatoes, cucumber, feta cheese, and Kalamata olives.
2. Drizzle olive oil over the salad and gently toss until all ingredients are well-coated.
3. Add salt and pepper to taste. Serve immediately or refrigerate for a chilled option.

TIP: For an extra burst of flavor, add a squeeze of fresh lemon juice or sprinkle some dried oregano on top before serving!

Stuffed Bell Peppers

PREPARATION TIME: 10 MINUTES

COOKING TIME: 25-30 MINUTES

SERVES: 4

Nutrition Information (Per Serving):
200 Calories / 6g Fat / 28g Carbohydrates / 8g Protein / 250mg Sodium / 4g Sugar

INGREDIENTS:

- 4 large bell peppers (any color), tops cut off and seeds removed
- 1 cup quinoa, cooked according to package instructions
- 1/2 cup canned black beans, drained and rinsed
- 1/2 cup cherry tomatoes, diced
- 1/4 cup feta cheese, crumbled

*Salt and pepper, to taste

DIRECTIONS:

1. Preheat your oven to 375°F (190°C).
2. In a large bowl, combine the cooked quinoa, black beans, cherry tomatoes, and crumbled feta cheese. Season with salt and pepper to taste, and mix well.
3. Fill each bell pepper with the quinoa mixture, pressing it down gently to ensure the filling is packed.
4. Place the stuffed peppers upright in a baking dish. Bake in the preheated oven for 25-30 minutes, or until the peppers are tender and the filling is heated through.
5. Remove from the oven, let cool slightly, and serve warm with a side of Greek yogurt or a drizzle of tzatziki sauce for extra tangy flavor!

Lentil Soup

PREPARATION TIME: 10 MINUTES

COOKING TIME: 30 -35 MINUTES

SERVES: 4

Nutrition Information (Per Serving):
110 Calories / 9g Fat / 4g Carbohydrates / 4g Protein / 220mg Sodium / 1g Sugar

INGREDIENTS:

- 1 cup dried lentils, rinsed
- 1 medium onion, finely chopped
- 2 medium carrots, diced
- 4 cups vegetable broth
- 2 celery stalks, diced

*Olive oil, for sautéing
*Salt and pepper, to taste
*Chopped fresh parsley for garnish (optional)

DIRECTIONS:

1. In a large pot, heat a drizzle of olive oil over medium heat. Add the chopped onion, diced carrots, and celery. Sauté for 5-7 minutes, or until the vegetables are softened.
2. Stir in the rinsed lentils and pour in the vegetable broth. Bring the mixture to a boil.
3. Reduce the heat to low, cover the pot, and let the soup simmer for 25-30 minutes, or until the lentils are tender.
4. Season with salt and pepper to taste, adjusting as needed.
5. Ladle the soup into bowls and garnish with chopped fresh parsley if desired.
6. Serve hot with a side of crusty bread.

Mediterranean Stuffed Avocados

 PREPARATION TIME: 10 MINUTES

 COOKING TIME: NONE

 SERVES: 4

Nutrition Information (Per Serving):
210 Calories / 15g Fat / 12g Carbohydrates / 5g Protein / 250mg Sodium / 2g Sugar

INGREDIENTS:

- 2 large avocados, halved and pitted
- 1/2 cup cherry tomatoes, diced
- 1/4 cup cucumber, diced
- 1/4 cup feta cheese, crumbled
- 2 tablespoons Kalamata olives, sliced

*Salt and pepper, to taste

DIRECTIONS:

1. Scoop out a small amount of the avocado flesh to create a larger well for the filling.
2. In a bowl, combine the diced cherry tomatoes, cucumber, feta cheese, and Kalamata olives.
3. Spoon the Mediterranean mixture evenly into the avocado halves.
4. Sprinkle with salt and pepper to taste, and serve immediately.

TIP: Add a squeeze of fresh lemon juice over the avocados to keep them from browning and to enhance the flavor!

Caprese Salad

 PREPARATION TIME: 10 MINUTES

COOKING TIME: NONE

 SERVES: 4

Nutrition Information (Per Serving):
200 Calories / 16g Fat / 6g Carbohydrates / 7g Protein / 150mg Sodium / 4g Sugar

INGREDIENTS:

- 3-4 large ripe tomatoes, sliced
- 1 pound fresh mozzarella cheese, sliced
- 1/4 cup fresh basil leaves
- 2 tablespoons extra virgin olive oil

*Salt and pepper, to taste

DIRECTIONS:

1. Arrange the tomato slices and mozzarella slices alternately on a large platter, slightly overlapping them.
2. Tuck fresh basil leaves between the tomato and mozzarella slices.
3. Drizzle the salad with extra virgin olive oil.
4. Season with salt and pepper, to taste.
5. Serve the salad immediately.

TIP: Drizzle a little balsamic glaze over the Caprese salad for an extra burst of flavor!

Garlic Lemon Shrimp Skewers

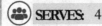

PREPARATION TIME: 10 MINUTES

COOKING TIME: 5-7 MINUTES (+15 minutes for marination)

SERVES: 4

Nutrition Information (Per Serving):
150 Calories / 8g Fat / 3g Carbohydrates / 20g Protein / 220mg Sodium / 1g Sugar

INGREDIENTS:

- 1 pound large shrimp, peeled and deveined
- 2 tablespoons olive oil
- 2 cloves garlic, minced
- 1 lemon, juiced
- 1 tablespoon fresh parsley, chopped

*Salt and pepper, to taste

DIRECTIONS:

1. If using wooden skewers, soak them in water for at least 15 minutes to prevent them from burning on the grill.
2. In a bowl, combine the olive oil, minced garlic, lemon juice, and chopped parsley. Add the shrimp, season with salt and pepper, and toss to coat evenly. Let the shrimp marinate for 15 minutes to absorb the flavors.
3. Thread the marinated shrimp onto the soaked skewers.
4. Preheat a grill or grill pan over medium-high heat. Cook the shrimp skewers for about 2-3 minutes on each side, or until the shrimp are pink and opaque.
5. Remove from the grill and serve immediately with a wedge of lemon on the side.

Avgolemono (Greek Lemon Chicken Soup)

PREPARATION TIME: 10 MINUTES

COOKING TIME: 30 MINUTES

SERVES: 4

Nutrition Information (Per Serving):
180 Calories / 8g Fat / 12g Carbohydrates / 15g Protein / 320mg Sodium / 1g Sugar

INGREDIENTS:

- 4 cups chicken broth
- 1/2 cup white rice (or orzo)
- 2 large eggs
- 1 lemon, juiced
- 1 cup cooked chicken, shredded

*Salt and pepper to taste
*Chopped fresh dill for garnish (optional)
*Lemon wedges for serving (optional)

DIRECTIONS:

1. In a large pot, bring the chicken broth to a boil. Add the rice (or orzo) and cook until tender, about 15-20 minutes.
2. While the rice is cooking, whisk the eggs and lemon juice together in a medium bowl until well combined.
3. Slowly add a ladle of hot broth to the egg-lemon mixture while whisking continuously to prevent the eggs from curdling.
4. Pour the tempered egg mixture back into the pot with the rice and broth, stirring constantly over low heat until the soup thickens slightly (do not let it boil).
5. Stir in the shredded chicken, season with salt and pepper to taste, and serve hot.

Piyaz (Turkish White Bean Salad)

PREPARATION TIME: 15 MINUTES

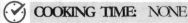
COOKING TIME: NONE

SERVES: 4

Nutrition Information (Per Serving):
200 Calories / 10g Fat / 20g Carbohydrates / 6g Protein / 400mg Sodium / 3g Sugar

INGREDIENTS:

- 2 cans (15 oz) white beans, drained
- 1 small red onion, thinly sliced
- 1/2 cup chopped fresh parsley
- 1/2 cup halved cherry tomatoes
- 1/4 cup olive oil

*Salt and pepper, to taste
*1 tablespoon lemon juice for a zesty twist (optional)

DIRECTIONS:

1. In a large bowl, mix the cooked white beans, halved cherry tomatoes, and thinly sliced red onion.
2. Stir in the chopped fresh parsley.
3. Drizzle olive oil over the mixture and toss gently to coat.
4. Season with salt and pepper to taste. If desired, add a drizzle of lemon juice for a zesty twist. Serve immediately or chill for enhanced flavor.

Hummus and Pomegranate Bulgur Bowl

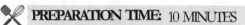
PREPARATION TIME: 10 MINUTES

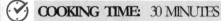
COOKING TIME: 30 MINUTES

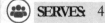
SERVES: 4

Nutrition Information (Per Serving):
290 Calories / 12g Fat / 34g Carbohydrates / 8g Protein / 220mg Sodium / 4g Sugar

INGREDIENTS:

- 1 cup bulgur, cooked according to package instructions
- 1/2 cup hummus (see recipe on p. 36)
- 1/4 cup pomegranate seeds
- 2 tablespoons fresh parsley, chopped
- 2 tablespoons olive oil

*Salt and pepper, to taste

DIRECTIONS:

1. Prepare the bulgur according to the package instructions and let it cool slightly.
2. In a serving bowl, layer the cooked bulgur as the base. Top with a generous scoop of hummus.
3. Sprinkle the pomegranate seeds and chopped parsley over the hummus and bulgur.
4. Drizzle olive oil over the entire bowl and season with salt and pepper to taste.
5. Serve the Hummus and Pomegranate Bulgur Bowl at room temperature or slightly chilled.

TIP: For an extra burst of flavor, add a handful of chopped nuts or a drizzle of lemon juice!

Herbed Turkey Meatballs

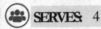 **PREPARATION TIME:** 10 MINUTES

COOKING TIME: 15-20 MINUTES

SERVES: 4

Nutrition Information (Per Serving):
180 Calories / 9g Fat / 6g Carbohydrates / 20g Protein / 320mg Sodium / 1g Sugar

INGREDIENTS:

- 1 pound ground turkey
- 1/4 cup bread crumbs
- 1/4 cup grated Parmesan cheese
- 1 egg
- 1 tablespoon dried Italian herbs (or a mix of oregano, basil, and thyme)

*Salt and pepper, to taste

DIRECTIONS:

1. Set your oven to 375°F (190°C).
2. In a large bowl, combine ground turkey, bread crumbs, Parmesan cheese, egg, dried Italian herbs, salt, and pepper. Mix until all ingredients are well incorporated.
3. Shape the mixture into small meatballs, about 1 inch in diameter.
4. Arrange the meatballs on a baking sheet lined with parchment paper. Bake for 15-20 minutes or until they are cooked through and golden brown.
5. Enjoy the meatballs hot with your favorite dipping sauce or over a bed of pasta or salad of your choice.

Zucchini Soup

PREPARATION TIME: 10 MINUTES

COOKING TIME: 20 MINUTES

SERVES: 4

Nutrition Information (Per Serving):
120 Calories / 7g Fat / 11g Carbohydrates / 3g Protein / 320mg Sodium / 4g Sugar

INGREDIENTS:

- 4 medium zucchinis, chopped
- 1 medium onion, chopped
- 2 cloves garlic, minced
- 4 cups vegetable broth
- 2 tablespoons olive oil

*Salt and pepper, to taste
*Fresh mint or basil, for garnish (optional)

DIRECTIONS:

1. In a large pot, heat the olive oil over medium heat. Add the chopped onion and minced garlic, sautéing for 3-4 minutes until softened and fragrant.
2. Add the chopped zucchini to the pot and cook for another 5 minutes, stirring occasionally.
3. Pour in the vegetable broth and bring the mixture to a boil. Reduce the heat to low and let it simmer for about 15 minutes, or until the zucchini is tender.
4. Using an immersion blender or a regular blender, blend the soup until smooth and creamy.
5. Season with salt and pepper to taste. Serve hot, garnished with fresh mint or basil leaves for a refreshing touch.

TIP: For a creamy texture and added richness, stir in a spoonful of Greek yogurt just before serving!

Greek Salad

PREPARATION TIME: 10 MINUTES

COOKING TIME: NONE

SERVES: 4

Nutrition Information (Per Serving):
150 Calories / 12g Fat / 9g Carbohydrates / 3g Protein / 500mg Sodium / 4g Sugar

INGREDIENTS:

- 1 cup halved cherry tomatoes
- 1 cup diced cucumber
- 1/4 cup sliced red onion
- 1/4 cup Kalamata olives
- 1/4 cup crumbled feta cheese

Dressing:
*olive oil and lemon juice (optional)
*Salt and pepper, to taste

DIRECTIONS:

1. In a large bowl, combine the halved cherry tomatoes, diced cucumber, and sliced red onion.
2. Stir in the Kalamata olives and crumbled feta cheese.
3. Drizzle with a little olive oil and a squeeze of lemon juice if desired. Season with salt and pepper to taste.
4. Toss the salad gently to combine and serve immediately.

Spicy Shrimp and Avocado Salad

PREPARATION TIME: 10 MINUTES

COOKING TIME: 5-7 MINUTES

SERVES: 4

Nutrition Information (Per Serving):
250 Calories / 15g Fat / 10g Carbohydrates / 20g Protein / 280mg Sodium / 2g Sugar

INGREDIENTS:

- 1 pound large shrimp, peeled and deveined
- 1 avocado, diced
- 1/2 cup cherry tomatoes, halved
- 2 tablespoons olive oil
- 1/2 teaspoon red pepper flakes

*Salt and pepper, to taste

DIRECTIONS:

1. In a skillet, heat the olive oil over medium-high heat. Add the shrimp and sprinkle with red pepper flakes. Cook for 2-3 minutes on each side or until the shrimp are pink and fully cooked.
2. In a large bowl, combine the cooked shrimp, diced avocado, and cherry tomatoes.
3. Drizzle a bit of olive oil over the salad and gently toss to combine.
4. Season with salt and pepper to taste, and serve immediately.

TIP: For an extra burst of flavor, squeeze fresh lime juice over the salad just before serving!

Grilled Chicken with Tzatziki Sauce

 **PREPARATION TIME:** 10 MINUTES

COOKING TIME: 15 MINUTES (+15 minutes for marination

SERVES: 4

Nutrition Information (Per Serving):
250 Calories / 12g Fat / 4g Carbohydrates / 28g Protein / 180mg Sodium / 1g Sugar

INGREDIENTS:

- 4 chicken breasts, cut into thin fillets
- 1 cup tzatziki sauce (see the recipe on p. 36)
- 1 lemon, juiced
- 2 tablespoons olive oil
- 1 tablespoon fresh dill (or 1 teaspoon dried dill)

*Salt and pepper, to taste

DIRECTIONS:

1. In a bowl, combine the lemon juice, olive oil, dill, salt, and pepper. Add the chicken fillets to the mixture and let them marinate for at least 15 minutes.
2. While the chicken is marinating, preheat the grill to medium-high heat.
3. Place the chicken fillets on the grill and cook for about 5-7 minutes on each side, or until fully cooked and no longer pink in the center.
4. The chicken from the grill and serve immediately with a side of tzatziki sauce for dipping.

Spinach and Cheese Stuffed Mushrooms

PREPARATION TIME: 10 MINUTES

COOKING TIME: 15-20 MINUTES

SERVES: 4

Nutrition Information (Per Serving):
160 Calories / 12g Fat / 5g Carbohydrates / 7g Protein / 150mg Sodium / 2g Sugar

INGREDIENTS:

- 12 large white mushrooms, stems removed
- 1 cup fresh spinach, chopped
- 1/2 cup cream cheese, softened
- 1/4 cup grated Parmesan cheese
- 2 tablespoons olive oil

*Salt and pepper, to taste

DIRECTIONS:

1. Preheat your oven to 375°F (190°C).
2. In a skillet, heat 1 tablespoon of olive oil over medium heat. Add the chopped spinach and sauté until wilted. Remove from heat and mix in the cream cheese, grated Parmesan, salt, and pepper.
3. Lightly brush the mushroom caps with the remaining olive oil. Fill each mushroom cap with the spinach and cheese mixture.
4. Arrange the stuffed mushrooms on a baking sheet and bake for 15-20 minutes, or until the mushrooms are tender and the cheese is golden and bubbly.
5. Enjoy these stuffed mushrooms warm.

Zucchini Noodles with Pesto

 PREPARATION TIME: 10 MINUTES

 COOKING TIME: 10 MINUTES

 SERVES: 4

Nutrition Information (Per Serving):
220 Calories / 18g Fat / 10g Carbohydrates / 6g Protein / 120mg Sodium / 2g Sugar

INGREDIENTS:

- 3 medium zucchinis, spiralized into noodles
- 1/2 cup pesto sauce (see recipe on p.37)
- 1/2 cup cherry tomatoes, halved
- 2 tablespoons pine nuts
- 1/4 cup Parmesan cheese, grated

*Salt and pepper, to taste
*Basel for garnish (optional)

DIRECTIONS:

1. In a large skillet, heat a little olive oil over medium heat. Add the spiralized zucchini noodles and sauté for 2-3 minutes until they are just tender but still have a bite.
2. Add the pesto sauce to the skillet and toss the zucchini noodles until they are evenly coated.
3. Add the Toppings: Stir in the cherry tomatoes and sprinkle with pine nuts.
4. Remove from heat and garnish with grated Parmesan cheese. Season with salt and pepper to taste.

Roasted Bell Pepper and Mozzarella Panini

 PREPARATION TIME: 10 MINUTES

 COOKING TIME: 8 MINUTES

SERVES: 4

Nutrition Information (Per Serving):
320 Calories / 18g Fat / 25g Carbohydrates / 12g Protein / 450mg Sodium

INGREDIENTS:

- 4 slices of your choice of bread
- 1/2 cup roasted bell peppers (jarred or homemade, sliced)
- 4 oz fresh mozzarella, sliced
- 1 tablespoon olive oil
- Fresh basil leaves (optional for garnish)

*Salt and pepper, to taste

DIRECTIONS:

1. If making homemade roasted bell peppers, preheat the oven to 450°F(230°C). Roast whole bell peppers on a baking sheet for 20-25 minutes, turning until charred. Transfer to a bowl, cover with plastic wrap, steam for 10 minutes, peel, seed, and slice.
2. Place slices of roasted bell peppers and mozzarella between two slices of bread. Add a few basil leaves if desired.
3. Lightly brush the outside of the bread with olive oil on both sides.
4. Heat a panini press, skillet, or grill pan over medium heat. Place the sandwich on the press or pan and cook until the bread is golden and crispy, and the mozzarella is melted, about 3-4 minutes per side.
5. Cut in half and enjoy warm.

Chapter ③

Snacks

Zucchini Fritters

 PREPARATION TIME: 10 MINUTES

 COOKING TIME: 15 MINURES

 SERVES: 4

Nutrition Information (Per Serving):
200 Calories / 20g Fat / 2g Carbohydrates / 3g Protein / 150mg Sodium / 0g Sugar

INGREDIENTS:

- 2 medium zucchinis, grated and drained
- 1/2 cup all-purpose flour
- 1 egg
- 1/4 cup grated Parmesan cheese
- 2 tablespoons olive oil

*Salt and pepper, to test

DIRECTIONS:

1. Grate the zucchinis and squeeze out any excess moisture using a clean cloth or paper towels.
2. In a large bowl, combine the grated zucchini, flour, egg, and Parmesan cheese. Stir until well mixed.
3. Heat the olive oil in a skillet over medium heat. Scoop about 2 tablespoons of the mixture into the skillet, flattening slightly to form a fritter. Repeat with the remaining mixture.
4. Cook each side for 2-3 minutes or until golden brown and crispy. Remove from the skillet and drain on paper towels.
5. Serve the fritters warm as a tasty snack with a dollop of Greek yogurt or a tangy tzatziki dip!

Tahini Sauce

 PREPARATION TIME: 10 MINUTES

 COOKING TIME: NONE

 SERVES: 4

Nutrition Information (Per Serving):
160 Calories / 14g Fat / 5g Carbohydrates / 4g Protein / 100mg Sodium / 0g Sugar

INGREDIENTS:

- 1/2 cup crushed sesame seeds
- 1/4 cup water (adjust for desired consistency)
- 2 tablespoons lemon juice
- 1 garlic clove, minced

*Salt and pepper, to test

DIRECTIONS:

1. In a bowl, whisk together the crushed sesame seeds and lemon juice until well combined.
2. Gradually add water, whisking until the sauce reaches your desired consistency.
3. Stir in the minced garlic and salt and pepper, to taste.
4. Serve immediately or refrigerate in an airtight container.

TIP: Tahini sauce is perfect as a dip for veggies, a drizzle over salads, or a flavorful spread on sandwiches and wraps!

Roasted Chickpeas

 PREPARATION TIME: 5 MINUTES

 COOKING TIME: 25-30 MINUTES

SERVES: 4

Nutrition Information (Per Serving):
150 Calories / 7g Fat / 18g Carbohydrates / 5g Protein / 180mg Sodium / 1g Sugar

INGREDIENTS:

- 1 can (15 oz) chickpeas, drained and rinsed
- 2 tablespoons olive oil
- 1 teaspoon paprika
- 1/2 teaspoon garlic powder

*Salt, to taste

DIRECTIONS:

1. Preheat your oven to 400°F (200°C).
2. Pat the chickpeas dry with a paper towel, then toss them in a bowl with olive oil, paprika, garlic powder, and salt until evenly coated.
3. Spread the chickpeas in a single layer on a baking sheet. Roast for 25-30 minutes, shaking the pan halfway through, until they are crispy and golden brown.
4. Let the chickpeas cool slightly before serving as a crunchy snack or topping for salads.

TIP: Store roasted chickpeas in an airtight container to keep them crispy for up to 3 days!

Roasted Red Pepper Dip

 PREPARATION TIME: 10 MINUTES

 COOKING TIME: 5 MINUTES (if roasting peppers yourself)

 SERVES: 4

Nutrition Information (Per Serving):
150 Calories / 10g Fat / 13g Carbohydrates / 3g Protein / 200mg Sodium / 4g Sugar

INGREDIENTS:

- 2 large roasted red peppers (jarred or homemade)
- 1/2 cup Greek yogurt
- 1 clove garlic, minced
- 2 tablespoons olive oil
- 1 teaspoon smoked paprika

*Salt and pepper, to taste

DIRECTIONS:

1. If making homemade roasted bell peppers, preheat the oven to 450°F (230°C). Place whole bell peppers on a baking sheet and roast for 20-25 minutes, turning occasionally until charred. Transfer the roasted peppers to a bowl, cover with plastic wrap, and let them steam for 10 minutes. Once cooled, peel, seed, and slice the peppers.
2. In a food processor, combine the roasted red peppers, Greek yogurt, minced garlic, olive oil, smoked paprika, salt, and pepper. Blend until the mixture is smooth and creamy.
3. Taste the dip and adjust the seasoning by adding more salt and pepper, if needed. Blend again to ensure everything is well combined.
4. Transfer the dip to a serving bowl and enjoy with pita bread, crackers, or fresh veggies as a delicious snack!

Watermelon and Feta Salat

 PREPARATION TIME: 10 MINUTES

COOKING TIME: NONE

SERVES: 4

Nutrition Information (Per Serving):
90 Calories / 4g Fat / 12g Carbohydrates / 3g Protein / 160mg Sodium / 9g Sugar

INGREDIENTS:

- 4 cups watermelon, cubed
- 1 cup feta cheese, crumbled
- 1/4 cup fresh mint leaves, chopped
- 2 tablespoons olive oil
- 1 tablespoon balsamic glaze or balsamic vinegar

DIRECTIONS:

1. In a large bowl, combine the watermelon cubes, crumbled feta, and chopped mint.
2. Drizzle with olive oil and balsamic glaze or balsamic vinegar.
3. Toss gently to combine.
4. Serve immediately and enjoy a refreshing and flavorful snack.

TIP: For an extra burst of flavor, add a squeeze of fresh lime juice!

Mediterranean Deviled Eggs

 PREPARATION TIME: 15 MINUTES

 COOKING TIME: 10 MINUTES

 SERVES: 4

Nutrition Information (Per Serving):
110 Calories / 8g Fat / 2g Carbohydrates / 6g Protein / 240mg Sodium / 1g Sugar

INGREDIENTS:

- 6 large eggs, hard-boiled
- 1/4 cup Greek yogurt
- 1/4 cup Kalamata olives, finely chopped
- 1 tablespoon Dijon mustard
- 1 teaspoon paprika (for garnish)

DIRECTIONS:

1. Peel the hard-boiled eggs and slice them in half lengthwise. Remove the yolks and place them in a bowl.
2. Mash the egg yolks with a fork, then mix in the Greek yogurt, chopped Kalamata olives, and Dijon mustard until smooth.
3. Spoon the yolk mixture back into the egg whites, mounding it slightly.
4. Sprinkle the filled eggs with paprika for a touch of color and serve immediately.

TIP: For an extra burst of flavor, add a sprinkle of fresh herbs like dill or parsley on top before serving!

Herbed Goat Cheese with Crackers

PREPARATION TIME: 5 MINUTES

COOKING TIME: NONE

SERVES: 4

Nutrition Information (Per Serving):
150 Calories / 11g Fat / 5g Carbohydrates / 7g Protein / 180mg Sodium / 1g Sugar

INGREDIENTS:

- 1 log (4 oz) goat cheese
- 1 tablespoon fresh parsley, chopped
- 1 tablespoon fresh dill, chopped
- 1 tablespoon olive oil
- Crackers (for serving)

DIRECTIONS:

1. In a small bowl, mix the chopped parsley, dill, and olive oil until well combined.
2. Roll the goat cheese log in the herb mixture, pressing gently to ensure the herbs stick to the cheese.
3. Arrange the herbed goat cheese on a serving plate with crackers on the side.

TIP: For added flavor, drizzle a little honey over the goat cheese before serving!

Labneh (Thickened Yogurt)

PREPARATION TIME: 5 MINUTES

DRAINING TIME: 12-24 HOURS

SERVES: 4

Nutrition Information (Per Serving):
100 Calories / 5g Fat / 6g Carbohydrates / 8g Protein / 120mg Sodium / 4g Sugar

INGREDIENTS:

- 4 cups plain full-fat Greek yogurt (or regular yogurt)
- 1 teaspoon salt
- Cheesecloth or a clean kitchen towel

DIRECTIONS:

1. In a bowl, mix the yogurt with the salt until well combined.
2. Place the cheesecloth or clean kitchen towel over a fine-mesh strainer or colander, then set it over a large bowl. Pour the salted yogurt into the cloth.
3. Gather the edges of the cloth and tie them together to form a bundle. Let the yogurt drain in the refrigerator for 12-24 hours, or until it reaches your desired consistency. The longer it drains, the thicker the labneh will be.
4. Once the labneh is ready, transfer it to a bowl and store it in an airtight container in the refrigerator.

TIP: Enjoy labneh with warm pita bread, fresh veggies, or as a spread on toast. It's also perfect as a base for dipping with olive oil and herbs!

Greek Tzatziki Dip

PREPARATION TIME: 10 MINUTES

COOKING TIME: NONE

CHILLING TIME: 15 MINUTES

SERVES: 4

Nutrition Information (Per Serving):
100 Calories / 6g Fat / 6g Carbohydrates / 4g Protein / 60mg Sodium / 4g Sugar

INGREDIENTS:

- 1 cup Greek yogurt
- 1/2 cucumber, grated and drained
- 1 clove garlic, minced
- 1 tablespoon lemon juice
- 1 tablespoon fresh dill, chopped

*Salt and pepper, to test

DIRECTIONS:

1. Grate the cucumber and squeeze out excess water using a clean kitchen towel or paper towels.
2. In a medium bowl, mix the Greek yogurt, grated cucumber, minced garlic, lemon juice, and chopped dill.
3. Stir until all the ingredients are well combined. Season with salt and pepper to taste if desired.
4. Refrigerate for at least 15 minutes before serving to allow the flavors to meld.
5. Serve chilled with pita bread, fresh vegetables, or as a sauce for grilled meats.

TIP: For an extra burst of flavor, add a drizzle of olive oil on top before serving!

Hummus with Olive Oil and Paprika

PREPARATION TIME: 10 MINUTES

COOKING TIME: 5 MINUTES

SERVES: 4

Nutrition Information (Per Serving):
180 Calories / 12g Fat / 14g Carbohydrates / 6g Protein / 240mg Sodium / 1g Sugar

INGREDIENTS:

- 1 can (15 oz) chickpeas, drained and rinsed
- 1/4 cup tahini (see recipe on p. 32)
- 2 tablespoons lemon juice
- 2 tablespoons olive oil (plus extra for drizzling)
- 1/2 teaspoon paprika (for garnish)

DIRECTIONS:

1. In a food processor, combine the chickpeas, tahini, lemon juice, and 2 tablespoons of olive oil. Blend until smooth, adding a little water if needed to reach your desired consistency.
2. Transfer the hummus to a serving bowl. Drizzle with extra olive oil and sprinkle with paprika.
3. Enjoy your hummus fresh with pita bread, veggies, or as a spread.

TIP: Store the hummus in an airtight container in the refrigerator for up to 5 days. To keep it fresh, drizzle a thin layer of olive oil on top before sealing!

Simple Pesto

 PREPARATION TIME: 10 MINUTES

 COOKING TIME: NONE

SERVES: 4

Nutrition Information (Per Serving):
200 Calories / 20g Fat / 2g Carbohydrates / 3g Protein / 150mg Sodium / 0g Sugar

INGREDIENTS:

- 2 cups fresh basil leaves
- 1/2 cup extra virgin olive oil
- 1/3 cup pine nuts or walnuts
- 2 cloves garlic, minced
- 1/2 cup grated Parmesan cheese

*Salt and pepper to taste

DIRECTIONS:

1. In a food processor, combine the basil leaves, nuts, and garlic. Pulse until finely chopped.
2. While the processor is running, slowly drizzle in the olive oil until the mixture is smooth.
3. Add the grated Parmesan cheese, and pulse until combined.
4. Season with salt, pepper.
5. Serve immediately or store in an airtight container in the refrigerator.

TIP: Use pesto on pasta, sandwiches, or drizzled over grilled veggies, chicken, or fish!

Spiced Nuts (Marcona Almonds)

 PREPARATION TIME: 5 MINUTES

 COOKING TIME: 10 MINUTES

SERVES: 4

Nutrition Information (Per Serving):
180 Calories / 15g Fat / 5g Carbohydrates / 4g Protein / 140mg Sodium / 1g Sugar

INGREDIENTS:

- 1 cup Marcona almonds
- 1 tablespoon olive oil
- 1 teaspoon smoked paprika
- 1/2 teaspoon sea salt
- 1/4 teaspoon cayenne pepper (optional, for heat)

DIRECTIONS:

1. Preheat your oven to 350°F (175°C).
2. In a bowl, toss the Marcona almonds with olive oil, smoked paprika, sea salt, and cayenne pepper until they are well-coated.
3. Spread the almonds in a single layer on a baking sheet and roast in the oven for about 8-10 minutes, stirring once halfway through, until they are golden and fragrant.
4. Let the almonds cool slightly before serving as a flavorful snack or topping for salads.

TIP: For an extra touch of sweetness, add a drizzle of honey to the almonds before roasting!

Baba Ganoush

 PREPARATION TIME: 10 MINUTES

 COOKING TIME: 30 MINUTES

 SERVES: 4

Nutrition Information (Per Serving):
120 Calories / 10g Fat / 8g Carbohydrates / 2g Protein / 150mg Sodium / 3g Sugar

INGREDIENTS:

- 2 medium eggplants
- 1/4 cup tahini (see recipe on p. 32)
- 2 tablespoons olive oil
- 2 cloves garlic, minced
- 2 tablespoons lemon juice

*Salt and pepper to taste
*Fresh parsley for garnish (optional)

DIRECTIONS:

1. Preheat the oven to 400°F (200°C). Pierce the eggplants with a fork and place them on a baking sheet. Roast for 35-40 minutes, until the skin is charred and the eggplant is soft. Let cool, then peel the skin off.
2. In a food processor, combine the roasted eggplant, tahini, olive oil, minced garlic, and lemon juice. Blend until smooth.
3. Taste and adjust with salt and pepper to your preference.
4. Garnish with chopped fresh parsley, if desired.
5. Pairs well with pita bread, crackers, or fresh vegetables.

Garlic and Herb Labneh Balls

 PREPARATION TIME: 10 MINUTES

 COOKING TIME: NONE

❄ **CHILLING TIME:** 2-4 HOURS

 SERVES: 4

Nutrition Information (Per Serving): 150 Calories / 11g Fat / 6g Carbohydrates / 5g Protein / 120mg Sodium / 2g Sugar

INGREDIENTS:

- 2 cups labneh (thickened yogurt) (see recipe on p. 35)
- 1 clove garlic, minced
- 2 tablespoons fresh herbs (like parsley, dill, or mint), chopped
- 2 tablespoons olive oil
- 1 teaspoon lemon zest

*Salt and pepper, to taste

DIRECTIONS:

1. In a bowl, combine the labneh, minced garlic, chopped fresh herbs, lemon zest, salt, and pepper. Mix well until fully incorporated.
2. Using your hands or a spoon, shape the labneh mixture into small balls, about the size of a walnut.
3. Place the labneh balls on a tray and refrigerate for 2-4 hours until they firm up.
4. Drizzle with olive oil and serve with pita bread, crackers, or fresh veggies.

TIP: Store the labneh balls in an airtight container in the refrigerator for up to 5 days. For extra freshness, keep them submerged in olive oil!

Marinated Olives

PREPARATION TIME: 10 MINUTES

COOKING TIME: 1-2 HOURS (or overnight for best flavor)

SERVES: 4-6

Nutrition Information (Per Serving):
150 Calories / 15g Fat / 2g Carbohydrates / 1g Protein / 300mg Sodium / 0g Sugar Ingredients:

INGREDIENTS:

- 2 cups mixed olives (Kalamata, green, and black)
- 1/4 cup olive oil
- 1 clove garlic, minced
- 1 teaspoon lemon zest
- 1 teaspoon dried oregano

DIRECTIONS:

1. In a bowl, mix olive oil, minced garlic, lemon zest, and dried oregano.
2. Add the mixed olives to the bowl and toss them in the marinade until well-coated.
3. Cover the bowl and refrigerate for at least 1 hour to allow the flavors to meld.
4. Serve chilled or at room temperature.

TIP: For extra flavor, add a pinch of crushed red pepper flakes for a bit of spice!

Baked Pita Chips with Hummus

PREPARATION TIME: 5 MINUTES

COOKING TIME: 10-12 MINUTES

SERVES: 4

Nutrition Information (Per Serving):
180 Calories / 9g Fat / 20g Carbohydrates / 4g Protein / 200mg Sodium / 1g Sugar

INGREDIENTS:

- 4 pita bread pockets, cut into triangles
- 2 tablespoons olive oil
- 1/2 teaspoon sea salt
- 1/2 teaspoon paprika
- 1 cup hummus (see recipe on p. 36)

DIRECTIONS:

1. Preheat your oven to 375°F (190°C).
2. Arrange the pita triangles on a baking sheet. Brush them lightly with olive oil, then sprinkle with sea salt and paprika.
3. Bake in the preheated oven for 10-12 minutes, or until the pita chips are golden brown and crispy.
4. Let the pita chips cool slightly, then serve them warm with a side of creamy hummus.

TIP: For added flavor, sprinkle some dried oregano or cumin on the pita chips before baking!

Stuffed Mini Bell Peppers

PREPARATION TIME: 10 MINUTES

COOKING TIME: 15 MINUTES

SERVES: 4

Nutrition Information (Per Serving):
120 Calories / 9g Fat / 5g Carbohydrates / 4g Protein / 140mg Sodium / 2g Sugar

INGREDIENTS:

- 12 mini bell peppers, halved and seeds removed
- 1/2 cup cream cheese, softened
- 1/4 cup feta cheese, crumbled
- 2 tablespoons fresh parsley, chopped
- 1 tablespoon olive oil

*Salt and pepper to taste

DIRECTIONS:

1. Preheat your oven to 375°F (190°C).
2. In a bowl, mix the softened cream cheese, crumbled feta cheese, and chopped parsley until well combined.
3. Fill each mini bell pepper half with the cheese mixture, pressing gently to ensure it's evenly distributed.
4. Arrange the stuffed peppers on a baking sheet, drizzle with olive oil, and bake for 15 minutes, or until the peppers are tender and the cheese is slightly golden.
5. Serve the stuffed mini bell peppers warm, paired with a side of tzatziki or your favorite dipping sauce for an extra burst of flavor!

Grilled Halloumi Cheese with Lemon

PREPARATION TIME: 5 MINUTES

COOKING TIME: NONE

SERVES: 4

Nutrition Information (Per Serving):
180 Calories / 14g Fat / 2g Carbohydrates / 10g Protein / 320mg Sodium / 1g Sugar

INGREDIENTS:

- 8 oz halloumi cheese, sliced into 1/2-inch thick pieces
- 1 lemon, sliced into wedges
- 2 tablespoons olive oil
- 1 teaspoon dried oregano

*Fresh parsley, for garnish (optional)

DIRECTIONS:

1. Heat your grill or grill pan over medium-high heat.
2. Brush both sides of the halloumi cheese slices with olive oil and sprinkle with dried oregano.
3. Place the halloumi slices on the grill and cook for 2-3 minutes on each side, or until grill marks appear and the cheese is golden brown.
4. Arrange the grilled halloumi on a platter with lemon wedges on the side. Squeeze the lemon juice over the hot cheese for a burst of freshness.
5. Optionally, sprinkle with fresh parsley before serving.

TIP: For an extra kick of flavor, drizzle the grilled halloumi with a bit of honey or balsamic glaze before serving!

Kolokithakia Tiganita (Fried Zucchini)

PREPARATION TIME: 10 MINUTES

COOKING TIME: 15 MINUTES

SERVES: 4

Nutrition Information (Per Serving):
250 Calories / 14g Fat / 28g Carbohydrates / 4g Protein / 250mg Sodium / 1g Sugar

INGREDIENTS:

- 2 medium zucchinis, thinly sliced
- 1 cup all-purpose flour
- 1/2 cup cold sparkling water (adjust for batter consistency)
- Olive oil, for frying

*Salt and pepper, to taste

DIRECTIONS:

1. In a bowl, mix the flour with cold sparkling water to create a smooth batter. The consistency should be similar to pancake batter, so adjust the water if necessary.
2. In a deep skillet or frying pan, heat olive oil over medium-high heat until hot but not smoking.
3. Dip the thin zucchini slices into the batter, ensuring they're well-coated.
4. Carefully place the battered zucchini slices into the hot oil. Fry for about 2-3 minutes on each side, or until golden and crispy.
5. Remove the fried zucchini from the oil and drain on paper towels. Sprinkle with salt and serve immediately.

TIP: Serve with a side of tzatziki for extra flavor!

Spanakopita Bites (Mini Spinach and Feta Pies)

PREPARATION TIME: 15 MINUTES

COOKING TIME: 20 MINUTES

SERVES: 4

Nutrition Information (Per Serving):
140 Calories / 10g Fat / 9g Carbohydrates / 5g Protein / 180mg Sodium / 1g Sugar

INGREDIENTS:

- 1 cup spinach, chopped (fresh or thawed frozen spinach, drained)
- 1/2 cup feta cheese, crumbled
- 1/4 cup ricotta cheese
- 12 sheets phyllo dough, cut into small squares
- 2 tablespoons olive oil

*Salt and pepper, to taste

DIRECTIONS:

1. In a bowl, combine the chopped spinach, crumbled feta cheese, ricotta cheese, salt, and pepper. Mix until well combined.
2. Brush each phyllo dough square with olive oil. Layer 3-4 squares on top of each other in a mini muffin tin, pressing gently to form a cup.
3. Spoon a small amount of the spinach and cheese mixture into each phyllo cup. Bake in a preheated oven at 375°F (190°C) for 15-20 minutes, or until the phyllo is golden and crispy.
4. Let the Spanakopita Bites cool slightly before serving as a delicious appetizer or snack.

Dolmas
(Stuffed Grape Leaves)

 **PREPARATION TIME:** 15 MINUTES

 COOKING TIME: 20-25 MINUTES

SERVES: 4

Nutrition Information (Per Serving):
180 Calories / 10g Fat / 18g Carbohydrates / 4g Protein /
350mg Sodium / 7g Sugar

INGREDIENTS:

- 1 jar (16 oz) grape leaves in brine, drained and rinsed
- 1 cup rice, uncooked
- 1/4 cup pine nuts
- 2 tablespoons olive oil
- 1 lemon, juiced

*Salt and pepper, to taste

DIRECTIONS:

1. In a large skillet, heat 2 tablespoons of olive oil over medium heat. Add the uncooked rice and pine nuts, stirring frequently for 2-3 minutes until the rice is lightly toasted and the pine nuts are golden. Remove from heat and stir in half of the lemon juice, salt, and pepper to taste. Mix well.

2. Drain and rinse the grape leaves thoroughly to remove excess brine. Lay a grape leaf flat, shiny side down. Add 1-2 teaspoons of the rice mixture near the stem end. Fold in the sides of the leaf and roll tightly like a burrito. Repeat with remaining grape leaves and rice mixture.

3. Line the bottom of a large pot with a few grape leaves to prevent sticking. Arrange the stuffed grape leaves seam-side down in the pot, packing them snugly in layers.

4. Drizzle the remaining lemon juice over the dolmas. Pour in enough water to cover the dolmas halfway. Place a heatproof plate on top of the grape leaves to prevent them from unrolling during cooking.

5. Bring to a gentle simmer over low heat and cook for about 60 minutes, until the rice is tender.

6. After cooking, let the dolmades cool to room temperature. When ready to serve, they can be enjoyed cold, which is traditional, or gently warmed up if you prefer.

TIP: For the best flavor, make the dolmades a day ahead and let them chill in the refrigerator overnight. This allows the flavors to meld and intensify, making them even more delicious when served the next day.

Mezze Platter

A mezze platter is a collection of small, flavorful dishes that are commonly enjoyed in Mediterranean and Middle Eastern cuisines. The term "mezze" refers to a variety of appetizers or small plates that are served together, creating a diverse and communal eating experience.

Mezze platters are often enjoyed as an appetizer before a main course but can also be served as a complete meal. The dishes on a mezze platter are designed to be shared, offering a range of tastes, textures, and aromas that complement each other.

A typical mezze platter may include items such as:

- **Greek Tzatziki Dip** (see recipe on p.36)
- **Hummus** (see recipe on p.36)
- **Baba Ghanoush** (see recipe on p.38)
- **Stuffed Grape Leaves (Dolmas)** (see recipe on p.42)
- **Pita bread, Crackers**
- **Assorted Fresh Vegetables**
- **Marinated Olives** (see recipe on p.39)
- **Feta Cheese**
- **Garlic and Herb Labneh Balls** (see recipe on p.38)
- **Spiced Nuts (Marcona Almonds)** (see recipe on p.37)
- **Various Salads of Your Choice**

The beauty of a mezze platter lies in its versatility—you can mix and match your favorite dishes to create a personalized and satisfying spread. Whether enjoyed with family, friends, or guests, a mezze platter is a wonderful way to experience the rich and diverse flavors of the Mediterranean and Middle Eastern regions.

Chapter ④

Dinner

Lemon Garlic Shrimp Pasta

 PREPARATION TIME: 10 MINUTES

 COOKING TIME: 15-20 MINUTES

SERVES: 4

Nutrition Information (Per Serving):
320 Calories / 12g Fat / 38g Carbohydrates / 18g Protein / 240mg Sodium / 2g Sugar

INGREDIENTS:

- 8 oz spaghetti
- 1/2 lb shrimp, peeled and deveined
- 2 tablespoons olive oil
- 2 cloves garlic, minced
- 1 lemon, juiced

*Salt and pepper, to taste

DIRECTIONS:

1. Cook the spaghetti according to the package instructions until al dente. Drain and set aside.
2. In a large skillet, heat olive oil over medium heat. Add the minced garlic and sauté for about 1 minute until fragrant. Add the shrimp and cook for 2-3 minutes on each side, or until they turn pink and are fully cooked.
3. Add the cooked spaghetti to the skillet with the shrimp. Pour in the lemon juice, and season with salt and pepper to taste. Toss to combine all the ingredients.
4. Serve the pasta warm, with a sprinkle of fresh herbs if desired.

Tomato Basil Risotto

 PREPARATION TIME: 10 MINUTES

 COOKING TIME: 25 MINUTES

SERVES: 4

Nutrition Information (Per Serving):
220 Calories / 8g Fat / 34g Carbohydrates / 5g Protein / 320mg Sodium / 2g Sugar

INGREDIENTS:

- 1 1/2 cups Arborio rice
- 4 cups vegetable broth
- 1 1/2 cups fresh cherry tomatoes, halved
- 1/4 cup fresh basil, chopped
- 2 tablespoons olive oil

*Salt and pepper, to taste

DIRECTIONS:

1. In a large pan, heat 2 tablespoons of olive oil over medium heat.
2. Add the halved cherry tomatoes to the pan and cook for about 4-5 minutes until softened and slightly blistered. Remove them from the pan and set aside.
3. In the same pan, add the Arborio rice and stir for 2-3 minutes to lightly toast the rice.
4. Gradually add the vegetable broth, 1/2 cup at a time, stirring constantly. Allow the liquid to absorb before adding more. Continue this process until the rice is tender and creamy (about 20-25 minutes).
5. Once the risotto is cooked, stir in the cooked cherry tomatoes and fresh basil. Season with salt and pepper to taste.

TIP: For a touch of creaminess, stir in a spoonful of grated Parmesan cheese before serving!

Mediterranean Chicken Skewers

✂ **PREPARATION TIME:** 15 MINUTES

🍲 **MARINATING TIME:** 30 MINUTES

✅ **COOKING TIME:** 10-15 MINUTES

👥 **SERVES:** 4

Nutrition Information (Per Serving): 280 Calories/14g Fat/8g Carbohydrates/30g Protein /320mg Sodium/1g Sugar

INGREDIENTS:

- 1 lb chicken breast, cut into 1-inch cubes
- 2 tablespoons olive oil
- 1 lemon, juiced
- 1 tablespoon dried oregano
- 1 red bell pepper, cut into 1-inch pieces

*Salt and pepper, to taste

DIRECTIONS:

1. In a bowl, combine the chicken cubes, olive oil, lemon juice, dried oregano, salt, and pepper. Mix well, then let it marinate in the refrigerator for at least 30 minutes.
2. Thread the marinated chicken and red bell pepper pieces alternately onto skewers.
3. Preheat a grill or grill pan over medium-high heat. Cook the skewers for 10-15 minutes, turning occasionally, until the chicken is fully cooked and has nice grill marks.
4. Serve the Mediterranean Chicken Skewers hot, garnished with a squeeze of fresh lemon juice if desired.

Herbed Salmon with Spinach

✂ **PREPARATION TIME:** 10 MINUTES

✅ **COOKING TIME:** 15-20 MINUTES (+15 minutes for marination

👥 **SERVES:** 4

Nutrition Information (Per Serving):
320 Calories / 18g Fat / 4g Carbohydrates / 30g Protein / 140mg Sodium / 1g Sugar

INGREDIENTS:

- 4 salmon fillets (5–6 oz each)
- 2 tablespoons olive oil
- 1 teaspoon dried mixed herbs (such as thyme, basil, or rosemary)
- 4 cups fresh spinach
- 2 tablespoons lemon juice

*Salt and pepper, to taste

DIRECTIONS:

1. Preheat your oven to 375°F (190°C).
2. In a small bowl, mix together half of the olive oil, dill, salt, and pepper. Coat the salmon fillets in the marinade and let them sit for 10-15 minutes.
3. Place the marinated salmon fillets on a baking sheet lined with parchment paper.
4. Bake the salmon in the preheated oven for 12-15 minutes, or until the fish flakes easily with a fork.
5. While the salmon is baking, heat a little olive oil in a skillet over medium heat. Add the fresh spinach and cook until wilted, about 2-3 minutes. Drizzle with lemon juice and season with salt and pepper.
6. Plate the salmon fillets on a bed of sautéed spinach and garnish with extra dill and lemon, if desired.

Baked Cod with Tomatoes

⚔ **PREPARATION TIME:** 10 MINUTES

⏱ **COOKING TIME:** 20 MINUTES

👥 **SERVES:** 4

Nutrition Information (Per Serving):
280 Calories / 15g Fat / 6g Carbohydrates / 30g Protein / 450mg Sodium / 3g Sugar.

INGREDIENTS:

- 4 cod fillets
- 2 cups cherry tomatoes, halved
- 1/2 cup Kalamata olives (optional for added flavor)
- 3 tablespoons olive oil
- 1 teaspoon smoked paprika (or regular paprika)

*Salt and pepper, to taste

DIRECTIONS:

1. Preheat your oven to 200°C (400°F).
2. Place the cod fillets in a baking dish and drizzle with olive oil. Sprinkle the fillets with smoked paprika, and season with salt and pepper to taste.
3. Scatter the halved cherry tomatoes and olives around the cod in the baking dish.
4. Bake for 20 minutes, or until the cod is cooked through and flakes easily with a fork.
5. Garnish with a drizzle of extra olive oil or fresh herbs if desired, and serve immediately.

Garlic Butter Scallops

⚔ **PREPARATION TIME:** 10 MINUTES

⏱ **COOKING TIME:** 5 MINUTES

👥 **SERVES:** 4

Nutrition Information (Per Serving):
220 Calories / 15g Fat / 6g Carbohydrates / 18g Protein / 400mg Sodium / 0g Sugar

INGREDIENTS:

- 1 lb large scallops, patted dry
- 3 tablespoons unsalted butter
- 4 cloves garlic, minced
- 2 tablespoons olive oil
- Juice of 1/2 lemon

*Salt and pepper to taste

DIRECTIONS:

1. Season the scallops with salt and pepper on both sides.
2. Heat 2 tablespoons of butter and the olive oil in a large skillet over medium-high heat. Add the scallops in a single layer and cook for 2-3 minutes on each side, until golden brown and opaque. Remove the scallops from the skillet and set aside.
3. In the same skillet, add the remaining tablespoon of butter and the minced garlic. Sauté for 1 minute until fragrant.
4. Add the lemon juice and stir to combine. Return the scallops to the skillet, tossing them in the garlic butter sauce to coat.
5. Serve immediately, garnished with lemon wedges, if desired.

TIP: Pair these scallops with a light salad, steamed vegetables, or a side of your choice of pasta.

Grilled Swordfish

✗ **PREPARATION TIME:**	10 MINUTES
🍲 **MARINATING TIME:**	15-30 MINUTES
⏲ **COOKING TIME:**	8-10 MINUTES
👥 **SERVES:**	4

Nutrition Information (Per Serving):
320 Calories / 14g Fat / 1g Carbohydrates / 44g Protein / 220mg Sodium / 0g Sugar

INGREDIENTS:

- 4 swordfish steaks (about 6 oz each)
- 2 tablespoons olive oil
- Juice of 1 lemon
- 2 cloves garlic, minced
- 2 teaspoons dried herbs (like dried thyme and oregano)

*Salt and pepper to taste
*Lemon wedges, for serving (optional)

DIRECTIONS:

1. In a small bowl, mix together olive oil, lemon juice, garlic, herbs, salt, and pepper.
2. Rub the mixture over both sides of the swordfish steaks. Let them marinate for 15-30 minutes.
3. Preheat the grill to medium-high heat and grill the swordfish steaks for 4-5 minutes per side, or until the fish is opaque and has nice grill marks.
4. Serve immediately, garnished with lemon wedges on the side, if desired.

Lahanodolmades (Stuffed Cabbage Rolls)

✗ **PREPARATION TIME:**	15 MINUTES
⏲ **COOKING TIME:**	40-45 MINUTES
👥 **SERVES:**	4-6

Nutrition Information (Per Serving):
280 Calories / 12g Fat / 22g Carbohydrates / 20g Protein / 250mg Sodium / 2g Sugar

INGREDIENTS:

- 1 large cabbage, leaves separated
- 1 lb ground beef (or lamb)
- 1/2 cup rice, uncooked
- 1 onion, finely chopped
- 1 lemon, juiced

*Salt and pepper, to taste

DIRECTIONS:

1. Boil a large pot of water and blanch the cabbage leaves for 2-3 minutes until they are soft and pliable. Remove and set aside.
2. In a large bowl, combine the ground beef, uncooked rice, chopped onion, salt, and pepper. Mix well until all ingredients are fully incorporated.
3. Place a spoonful of the filling in the center of each cabbage leaf. Fold in the sides and roll it up tightly like a burrito.
4. Arrange the stuffed cabbage rolls seam-side down in a large pot. Pour the lemon juice over the rolls and add enough water to cover them. Simmer over medium heat for 40-45 minutes or until the meat and rice are fully cooked.
5. Serve the Lahanodolmades warm. For an authentic touch, pair them with a dollop of Greek yogurt or tzatziki sauce!

Garlic and Herb Baked Cod

 PREPARATION TIME: 10 MINUTES

 COOKING TIME: 15-20 MINUTES

 SERVES: 4

Nutrition Information (Per Serving):
220 Calories / 9g Fat / 2g Carbohydrates / 32g Protein /
180mg Sodium / 1g Sugar

INGREDIENTS:

- 4 cod fillets (about 6 oz each)
- 2 tablespoons olive oil
- 2 cloves garlic, minced
- 1 tablespoon fresh parsley, chopped

*Salt and pepper, to taste

DIRECTIONS:

1. Preheat your oven to 400°F (200°C).
2. Place the cod fillets on a baking sheet lined with parchment paper. Drizzle with olive oil and sprinkle with minced garlic, chopped parsley, salt, and pepper.
3. Bake in the preheated oven for 15-20 minutes or until the fish is opaque and flakes easily with a fork.
4. Remove from the oven and serve the cod fillets warm, garnished with extra parsley if desired.

TIP: Pair the baked cod with a Greek salad or roasted vegetables of your choice.

Mediterranean Eggplant Bake

 PREPARATION TIME: 10 MINUTES

 COOKING TIME: 20-30 MINUTES

SERVES: 4

Nutrition Information (Per Serving):
250 Calories / 10g Fat / 6g Carbohydrates / 30g Protein /
500mg Sodium / 1g Sugar

INGREDIENTS:

- 2 medium eggplants, sliced into 1/2-inch rounds
- 1 cup marinara sauce
- 1/2 cup feta cheese, crumbled
- 2 tablespoons olive oil
- 1 tablespoon fresh basil, chopped (or 1 teaspoon dried basil)

*Salt and pepper, to taste

DIRECTIONS:

1. Preheat your oven to 400°F (200°C).
2. Arrange the eggplant slices on a baking sheet and drizzle with olive oil. Season with salt and pepper to taste.
3. Bake the eggplant in the preheated oven for 15 minutes, or until they begin to soften.
4. Remove the eggplant from the oven and spread a layer of marinara sauce over each slice. Sprinkle with crumbled feta cheese and chopped basil.
5. Return the eggplant to the oven and bake for an additional 10-15 minutes, until the cheese is slightly melted and the edges are golden brown.
6. Serve the Mediterranean Eggplant Bake warm.

Spinach and Feta Stuffed Chicken

 **PREPARATION TIME:** 15 MINUTES

COOKING TIME: 25-30 MINUTES

SERVES: 4

Nutrition Information (Per Serving):
320 Calories / 15g Fat / 3g Carbohydrates / 40g Protein /
480mg Sodium / 1g Sugar

INGREDIENTS:

- 4 boneless, skinless chicken breasts
- 1 cup fresh spinach, chopped
- 1/2 cup feta cheese, crumbled
- 2 cloves garlic, minced
- 1 tablespoon olive oil

*Salt and pepper to taste
*Toothpicks (for securing the chicken)

DIRECTIONS:

1. In a bowl, mix the chopped spinach, crumbled feta cheese, and minced garlic.
2. Open the butterflied chicken breasts and spoon the spinach and feta mixture into the center. Fold the chicken breasts back over to enclose the filling, securing with toothpicks if necessary.
3. Heat the olive oil in a large skillet over medium heat. Add the stuffed chicken breasts and cook for 5-7 minutes per side until golden brown. Transfer to a preheated oven at 375°F (190°C) and bake for an additional 15-20 minutes or until the chicken is cooked through.
4. Remove from the oven, let the chicken rest for a few minutes, then slice and serve warm.

Rosemary Lamb Chops

PREPARATION TIME: 10 MINUTES

COOKING TIME: 15-20 MINUTES

SERVES: 4

Nutrition Information (Per Serving):
320 Calories / 20g Fat / 1g Carbohydrates / 28g Protein /
400mg Sodium / 0g Sugar

INGREDIENTS:

- 8 lamb chops (about 1-inch thick)
- 2 tablespoons olive oil
- 2 cloves garlic, minced
- 2 tablespoons fresh rosemary, chopped (or 1 tablespoon dried rosemary)

*Salt and pepper to taste
*Lemon wedges, for serving (optional)

DIRECTIONS:

1. Preheat the oven to 400°F (200°C).
2. In a small bowl, mix the olive oil, garlic, rosemary, salt, and pepper.
3. Rub the rosemary mixture evenly over both sides of the lamb chops.
4. Heat a large ovenproof skillet over medium-high heat. Sear the lamb chops for 2-3 minutes per side until browned.
5. Transfer the skillet to the oven and roast for 8-10 minutes for medium-rare, or longer if desired.
6. Let the lamb chops rest for a few minutes before serving with lemon wedges.

TIP: Pair this dish with a light salad or grilled veggies drizzled with lemon.

Garlic Butter Shrimp with Asparagus

⚔ **PREPARATION TIME:** 10 MINUTES

⏲ **COOKING TIME:** 10-12 MINUTES

👥 **SERVES:** 4

Nutrition Information (Per Serving):
320 Calories / 22g Fat / 8g Carbohydrates / 24g Protein / 210mg Sodium / 2g Sugar

INGREDIENTS:

- 1 lb shrimp, peeled and deveined
- 1 bunch asparagus, trimmed and cut into 2-inch pieces
- 3 tablespoons butter
- 2 cloves garlic, minced
- 1 lemon, juiced

*Salt and pepper, to taste

DIRECTIONS:

1. In a large skillet, melt 1 tablespoon of butter over medium heat. Add the asparagus pieces and cook for 3-4 minutes until they are tender-crisp. Remove from the skillet and set aside.
2. In the same skillet, add the remaining butter and minced garlic. Sauté for about 1 minute until the garlic is fragrant. Add the shrimp and cook for 2-3 minutes on each side, or until they turn pink.
3. Return the asparagus to the skillet and drizzle with lemon juice. Stir everything together and cook for an additional 1-2 minutes, allowing the flavors to blend.
4. Season with salt and pepper to taste, and serve warm.

Calamari with Lemon and Garlic

⚔ **PREPARATION TIME:** 10 MINUTES

⏲ **COOKING TIME:** 5-7 MINUTES

👥 **SERVES:** 4

Nutrition Information (Per Serving):
200 Calories / 10g Fat / 4g Carbohydrates / 22g Protein / 380mg Sodium / 1g Sugar

INGREDIENTS:

- 1 lb calamari rings (cleaned)
- 2 tablespoons olive oil
- 2 cloves garlic, minced
- 1 lemon, juiced
- 1 tablespoon fresh parsley, chopped

*Salt and pepper, to taste

DIRECTIONS:

1. In a large skillet, heat the olive oil over medium-high heat.
2. Add the minced garlic to the skillet and sauté for about 1 minute until fragrant. Add the calamari rings and cook for 3-4 minutes, stirring frequently, until they are opaque and cooked through.
3. Drizzle the lemon juice over the calamari and sprinkle with chopped parsley. Season with salt and pepper to taste.
4. Remove from heat and serve immediately, garnished with extra parsley if desired.

TIP: For added flavor, pair the calamari with a side of tzatziki sauce or serve it over a bed of mixed greens!

Greek-Style Pork Tenderloin

🍴 PREPARATION TIME:	10 MINUTES	
🍲 MARINATING TIME:	1 HOUR	(optional for enhanced flavor)
⏱️ COOKING TIME:	20-25 MINUTES	
👥 SERVES:	4	

Nutrition Information (Per Serving):
320 Calories / 15g Fat / 2g Carbohydrates / 40g Protein / 350mg Sodium / 1g Sugar

INGREDIENTS:

- 1 lb pork tenderloin
- 2 tablespoons olive oil
- 1 tablespoon dried herb mix (such as oregano, thyme, and rosemary)
- 2 cloves garlic, minced
- 1 lemon, juiced

*Salt and pepper, to taste

DIRECTIONS:

1. In a small bowl, mix the olive oil, minced garlic, dried herb mix, lemon juice, salt, and pepper. Rub this mixture all over the pork tenderloin and let it marinate in the refrigerator for at least 1 hour.
2. Preheat your oven to 400°F (200°C).
3. Heat a skillet over medium-high heat and sear the pork tenderloin on all sides until it's browned, about 4-5 minutes.
4. Transfer the seared pork tenderloin to a baking dish and roast in the preheated oven for 15-20 minutes, or until the internal temperature reaches 145°F (63°C).
5. Let the pork rest for 5 minutes before slicing.

Lemon Herb Tilapia

🍴 PREPARATION TIME:	10 MINUTES	
🍲 MARINATING TIME:	10 -15 MINUTES	(optional but recommended)
⏱️ COOKING TIME:	10 -12 MINUTES	
👥 SERVES:	4	

Nutrition Information (Per Serving):
230 Calories / 11g Fat / 2g Carbohydrates / 30g Protein / 240mg Sodium / 0g Sugar

INGREDIENTS:

- 4 tilapia fillets (about 6 oz each)
- 2 tablespoons olive oil
- Juice and zest of 1 lemon
- 2 cloves garlic, minced
- 2 teaspoons dried herbs (like dried thyme and oregano)

*Salt and pepper, to taste
*Lemon wedges, for serving (optional)

DIRECTIONS:

1. Preheat the oven to 400°F (200°C). Lightly grease a baking dish or line it with parchment paper.
2. In a small bowl, mix together the olive oil, lemon juice, lemon zest, garlic, herbs, salt, and pepper.
3. Place the tilapia fillets in the prepared baking dish. Brush the lemon herb mixture over the fillets, ensuring they are evenly coated. Allow the fillets to marinate for 10-15 minutes for better flavor.
4. Place the baking dish in the preheated oven and bake for 10-12 minutes, or until the tilapia is opaque and flakes easily with a fork.
5. Remove from the oven and serve immediately, garnished with lemon wedges on the side, if desired.

Keftedes (Greek Meatballs)

PREPARATION TIME: 15 MINUTES

COOKING TIME: 20 MINUTES

SERVES: 4-6

Nutrition Information (Per Serving):
250 Calories / 14g Fat / 8g Carbohydrates / 22g Protein / 400mg Sodium / 2g Sugar

INGREDIENTS:

- 1 lb ground beef (or lamb)
- 1/2 cup breadcrumbs
- 1 small onion, finely chopped
- 1 egg
- 2 tablespoons fresh parsley, chopped (or 1 tablespoon dried parsley)

*Salt and pepper, to taste

DIRECTIONS:

1. In a large bowl, combine the ground beef, breadcrumbs, chopped onion, egg, parsley, salt, and pepper. Mix well until all ingredients are fully incorporated.
2. Form the mixture into small meatballs, about 1 inch in diameter.
3. Heat a skillet over medium heat with a little olive oil. Fry the meatballs in batches for about 6-8 minutes, turning them occasionally, until they are golden brown and cooked through.
4. Remove the meatballs from the skillet and drain on a paper towel-lined plate and served warm.

Lemon Garlic Turkey

PREPARATION TIME: 10 MINUTES

MARINATING TIME: 30 MINUTES (optional)

COOKING TIME: 25-30 MINUTES

SERVES: 4

Nutrition Information (Per Serving):
250 Calories / 12g Fat / 4g Carbohydrates / 30g Protein / 320mg Sodium / 1g Sugar

INGREDIENTS:

- 4 turkey breast cutlets (about 1 lb total)
- 3 tablespoons olive oil
- 3 cloves garlic, minced
- Juice and zest of 1 lemon
- 1 teaspoon dried oregano

*Salt and pepper to taste
*Fresh parsley, chopped, for garnish (optional)

DIRECTIONS:

1. In a small bowl, mix together the olive oil, minced garlic, lemon juice, lemon zest, oregano, salt, and pepper.
2. Coat the turkey cutlets with the marinade, ensuring they are well covered. Let them marinate in the refrigerator for at least 30 minutes, or longer if time allows.
3. Heat a skillet over medium-high heat. Add the turkey cutlets and cook for 4-5 minutes per side, or until the turkey is golden brown and cooked through.
4. Garnish with fresh parsley if desired.

TIP: This dish pairs well with roasted vegetables or a light salad.

Mediterranean Tuna Steak

PREPARATION TIME:	150 MINUTES
MARINATING TIME:	10 MINUTES
COOKING TIME:	8-10 MINUTES
SERVES:	4

Nutrition Information (Per Serving): 250 Calories/14g Fat /2g Carbohydrates/28g Protein/120mg Sodium/1g Sugar

INGREDIENTS:

- 4 tuna steaks (about 6 oz each)
- 2 tablespoons olive oil
- 2 teaspoons dried herbs (like dried thyme and oregano)
- 1 lemon, juiced
- 1 clove garlic, minced

*Salt and pepper, to taste

DIRECTIONS:

1. In a small bowl, mix the olive oil, lemon juice, minced garlic, dried herbs, salt, and pepper. Brush the mixture over the tuna steaks and let them marinate for at least 10 minutes.
2. Preheat a grill or skillet over medium-high heat.
3. Grill or sear the tuna steaks for about 3-4 minutes on each side, or until they reach your desired level of doneness.
4. Remove the tuna steaks from the heat and let them rest for a couple of minutes. Serve them warm with a garnish of lemon wedges if desired.

TIP: For extra flavor, serve the tuna steaks with a side of Greek salad or a drizzle of balsamic glaze!

Mediterranean Beef Stir-Fry

PREPARATION TIME:	10 MINUTES
COOKING TIME:	8-10 MINUTES
SERVES:	4

Nutrition Information (Per Serving):
180 Calories / 12g Fat / 8g Carbohydrates / 6g Protein / 220mg Sodium / 3g Sugar

INGREDIENTS:

- 1 pound beef strips (sirloin or flank steak recommended)
- 1 red bell pepper, sliced
- 1 zucchini, sliced
- 2 tablespoons olive oil
- 1 teaspoon dried oregano

*Salt and pepper, to taste

DIRECTIONS:

1. In a large skillet or wok, heat the olive oil over medium-high heat.
2. Add the beef strips to the skillet and stir-fry for about 5-7 minutes, or until browned and cooked through. Remove the beef from the skillet and set aside.
3. In the same skillet, add the sliced red bell pepper and zucchini. Stir-fry for about 5 minutes, or until the vegetables are tender but still crisp.
4. Return the cooked beef to the skillet with the vegetables. Sprinkle with dried oregano and season with salt and pepper to taste. Stir well to combine and cook for an additional 2-3 minutes to heat everything through.
5. Serve immediately as a flavorful Mediterranean dish.

Lemon and Caper Chicken Piccata

⚔ **PREPARATION TIME:** 10 MINUTES

🕑 **COOKING TIME:** 15-20 MINUTES

👥 **SERVES:** 4

Nutrition Information (Per Serving):
310 Calories / 14g Fat / 4g Carbohydrates / 38g Protein /
360mg Sodium / 1g Sugar

INGREDIENTS:

- 4 chicken breasts, thinly sliced
- 2 tablespoons olive oil
- 1/4 cup capers, drained
- 1 lemon, juiced
- 1/2 cup chicken broth

*Salt and pepper, to taste

DIRECTIONS:

1. Season the chicken breasts with salt and pepper on both sides.
2. In a large skillet, heat the olive oil over medium-high heat. Add the chicken breasts and cook for 3-4 minutes on each side, or until golden brown and cooked through. Remove the chicken from the skillet and set aside.
3. In the same skillet, add the chicken broth, lemon juice, and capers. Stir and let the mixture simmer for about 2-3 minutes, allowing the flavors to meld together.
4. Return the chicken breasts to the skillet, spooning the lemon-caper sauce over them. Let it cook for an additional 2-3 minutes to heat through.
5. Serve the Lemon and Caper Chicken Piccata warm with a side of your favorite vegetables or pasta.

Kofta Kebab

⚔ **PREPARATION TIME:** 15 MINUTES

🕑 **COOKING TIME:** 10 MINUTES

👥 **SERVES:** 4

Nutrition Information (Per Serving):
250 Calories / 15g Fat / 5g Carbohydrates / 25g Protein /
350mg Sodium / 1g Sugar

INGREDIENTS:

- 1 lb ground beef or lamb
- 1 small onion, finely grated
- 2 tablespoons fresh parsley, chopped
- 1 teaspoon ground cumin
- 1 teaspoon ground coriander

*Salt and pepper, to taste

DIRECTIONS:

1. In a large bowl, combine the ground beef or lamb with the grated onion, chopped parsley, ground cumin, ground coriander, salt, and pepper. Mix well until all the ingredients are evenly distributed.
2. Divide the mixture into equal portions and shape each portion into long, oval-shaped kebabs. You can either mold them around wooden or metal skewers or shape them by hand.
3. Preheat a grill or grill pan over medium-high heat. Grill the kebabs for about 4-5 minutes on each side, or until fully cooked through and slightly charred on the outside.
4. Remove the kebabs from the grill and serve hot with your favorite sides like rice, pita bread, or a light salad.

Sweet Potatoes with Hummus and Chickpeas

PREPARATION TIME: 10 MINUTES

COOKING TIME: 35-40 MINUTES

SERVES: 4

Nutrition Information (Per Serving):
300 Calories / 12g Fat / 42g Carbohydrates / 8g Protein /
350mg Sodium / 9g Sugar

INGREDIENTS:
- 2 large sweet potatoes, halved lengthwise
- 1 cup hummus (see recipe on p. 36)
- 1/2 cup canned chickpeas, drained and rinsed
- 1 tablespoon olive oil
- 1 teaspoon smoked paprika

*Salt and pepper to taste
*Fresh parsley, chopped, for garnish (optional)

DIRECTIONS:
1. Preheat your oven to 400°F (200°C).
2. Place the sweet potato halves on a baking sheet, drizzle with olive oil, and season with salt and pepper. Bake in the preheated oven for 35-40 minutes or until the sweet potatoes are tender and easily pierced with a fork.
3. While the sweet potatoes are baking, mix the chickpeas with a sprinkle of smoked paprika in a small bowl.
4. Once the sweet potatoes are done, spread a generous layer of hummus on each half. Top with the spiced chickpeas.
5. Garnish with chopped fresh parsley and a little extra smoked paprika if desired. Serve warm.

Mussels in White Sauce

PREPARATION TIME: 20 MINUTES

COOKING TIME: 10-12 MINUTES

SERVES: 4

Nutrition Information (Per Serving):
320 Calories / 18g Fat / 8g Carbohydrates / 26g Protein /
280mg Sodium / 2g Sugar

INGREDIENTS:
- 2 lbs mussels, cleaned and debearded
- 1/2 cup heavy cream
- 3 cloves garlic, minced
- 1/4 cup white wine (or vegetable broth)
- 2 tablespoons butter

*Salt and pepper, to taste

DIRECTIONS:
1. In a large pot, melt the butter over medium heat. Add the minced garlic and sauté for about 1 minute, until fragrant.
2. Pour in the white wine (or vegetable broth) and bring to a simmer.
3. Add the cleaned mussels to the pot, cover with a lid, and cook for 5-7 minutes, or until the mussels have opened. Discard any mussels that do not open.
4. Stir in the heavy cream and let it simmer for an additional 2-3 minutes until the sauce thickens slightly. Season with salt and pepper to taste.
5. Serve the mussels warm, drizzled with the creamy white sauce, alongside crusty bread for dipping.

Chapter 5

Side Dishes

Honey and Thyme Roasted Vegetables

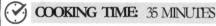
PREPARATION TIME: 10 MINUTES

COOKING TIME: 35 MINUTES

SERVES: 4

Nutrition Information (Per Serving):
180 Calories / 9g Fat / 25g Carbohydrates / 3g Protein / 250mg Sodium / 10g Sugar

INGREDIENTS:

- 4 cups of mixed vegetables (such as carrots, parsnips, sweet potatoes, and Brussels sprouts), cut into bite-sized pieces
- 2 tablespoons olive oil
- 2 tablespoons honey
- 1 tablespoon fresh thyme leaves (or 1 teaspoon dried thyme)

*Salt and pepper, to taste

DIRECTIONS:

1. Preheat your oven to 400°F (200°C).
2. In a large bowl, combine the mixed vegetables, olive oil, honey, thyme, salt, and pepper. Toss until the vegetables are evenly coated.
3. Spread the vegetables in a single layer on a baking sheet lined with parchment paper.
4. Roast in the preheated oven for 30-35 minutes, or until the vegetables are tender and caramelized, stirring halfway through for even cooking.
5. Serve hot, as a delicious and flavorful side dish.

Lemon Garlic Quinoa

PREPARATION TIME: 5 MINUTES

COOKING TIME: 15 MINUTES

SERVES: 4

Nutrition Information (Per Serving):
160 Calories / 6g Fat / 24g Carbohydrates / 5g Protein / 150mg Sodium / 1g Sugar

INGREDIENTS:

- 1 cup quinoa, rinsed
- 2 cups vegetable broth or water
- 2 tablespoons olive oil
- 2 cloves garlic, minced
- Zest and juice of 1 lemon

*Salt and pepper to taste
*Fresh parsley, chopped, for garnish (optional)

DIRECTIONS:

1. In a medium saucepan, combine the rinsed quinoa and vegetable broth or water. Bring to a boil over medium-high heat.
2. Reduce the heat to low, cover, and simmer for about 15 minutes, or until the quinoa is cooked and the liquid is absorbed. Remove from heat and let it sit, covered, for 5 minutes.
3. While the quinoa is cooking, heat the olive oil in a small skillet over medium heat. Add the minced garlic and sauté for 1-2 minutes until fragrant, being careful not to burn it.
4. Fluff the cooked quinoa with a fork and transfer it to a large bowl. Add the sautéed garlic, lemon zest, and lemon juice. Stir to combine.
5. Season with salt and pepper to taste.
6. Serve warm, garnished with chopped fresh parsley if desired.

Garlic Roasted Potatoes with Oregano

🍴 **PREPARATION TIME:** 10 MINUTES

⏱ **COOKING TIME:** 40 MINUTES

👥 **SERVES:** 4

Nutrition Information (Per Serving):
200 Calories / 10g Fat / 26g Carbohydrates / 4g Protein / 180mg Sodium / 2g Sugar

INGREDIENTS:

- 4 medium potatoes, cut into wedges
- 2 tablespoons olive oil
- 2 cloves garlic, minced
- 1 tablespoon dried oregano
- 1/2 cup vegetable broth or water

*Salt and pepper to taste
*Fresh parsley, chopped, for garnish (optional)

DIRECTIONS:

1. Preheat your oven to 400°F (200°C).
2. In a large bowl, combine the potato wedges, olive oil, minced garlic, dried oregano, salt, and pepper. Toss until the potatoes are evenly coated.
3. Place the potatoes in a single layer in a large baking dish.
4. Pour the vegetable broth or water around the potatoes in the dish.
5. Roast in the preheated oven for 40 minutes, stirring halfway through, until the potatoes are tender and golden brown.
6. Remove from the oven and garnish with chopped fresh parsley, if desired.

TIP: For extra flavor, sprinkle some freshly grated Parmesan cheese over the potatoes just before serving!

Simple Greek Rice Pilaf

🍴 **PREPARATION TIME:** 5 MINUTES

⏱ **COOKING TIME:** 20 MINUTES

👥 **SERVES:** 4

Nutrition Information (Per Serving):
220 Calories / 7g Fat / 35g Carbohydrates / 3g Protein / 250mg Sodium / 2g Sugar

INGREDIENTS:

- 1 cup long-grain rice (such as basmati or jasmine)
- 2 cups vegetable or chicken broth
- 1 small onion, finely chopped
- 2 tablespoons olive oil
- 1/4 cup fresh parsley, chopped (plus extra for garnish)

*Salt and pepper, to taste

DIRECTIONS:

1. In a medium saucepan, heat the olive oil over medium heat. Add the finely chopped onion and sauté until it becomes soft and translucent, about 3-4 minutes.
2. Add the rice to the saucepan and stir well, allowing it to toast slightly for about 2 minutes.
3. Pour in the vegetable or chicken broth. Stir to combine and bring the mixture to a boil.
4. Once boiling, reduce the heat to low, cover the saucepan, and let it simmer for about 15-20 minutes, or until the rice is tender and the liquid is absorbed.
5. Remove the saucepan from the heat. Fluff the rice with a fork, stir in the chopped parsley, and adjust seasoning with salt and pepper if desired.
6. Serve warm with an extra sprinkle of fresh parsley on top.

Grilled Asparagus with Lemon

🍴 **PREPARATION TIME:** 5 MINUTES

⏱ **COOKING TIME:** 10 MINUTES

👥 **SERVES:** 4

Nutrition Information (Per Serving):
80 Calories / 7g Fat / 5g Carbohydrates / 2g Protein / 150mg Sodium / 2g Sugar

INGREDIENTS:

- 1 bunch of asparagus, trimmed
- 2 tablespoons olive oil
- 1 lemon (zested and juiced)
- 2 cloves garlic, minced
- 1 tablespoon grated Parmesan cheese

*Salt and pepper to taste
*Fresh parsley, chopped, for garnish (optional)

DIRECTIONS:

1. Preheat your grill to medium-high heat.
2. In a large bowl, toss the asparagus with olive oil, minced garlic, lemon zest, salt, and pepper until evenly coated.
3. Place the asparagus on the grill in a single layer and cook for 3-4 minutes on each side, until tender and slightly charred.
4. Remove the asparagus from the grill and drizzle with fresh lemon juice.
5. Sprinkle with grated Parmesan cheese and garnish with chopped fresh parsley before serving, if desired.

Broccoli with Lemon and Garlic

🍴 **PREPARATION TIME:** 5 MINUTES

⏱ **COOKING TIME:** 10 MINUTES

👥 **SERVES:** 4

Nutrition Information (Per Serving):
90 Calories / 6g Fat / 9g Carbohydrates / 3g Protein / 120mg Sodium / 2g Sugar

INGREDIENTS:

- 1 large head of broccoli, cut into florets
- 2 tablespoons olive oil
- 3 cloves garlic, thinly sliced
- Juice and zest of 1 lemon

*Salt and black pepper, to taste

DIRECTIONS:

1. Steam or blanch the broccoli florets until they are tender but still crisp, about 5-7 minutes. Drain and set aside.
1. In a large skillet, heat the olive oil over medium heat. Add the garlic and sauté until fragrant, about 1-2 minutes.
2. Add the broccoli to the skillet and toss well with the garlic and olive oil.
3. Drizzle with lemon juice, sprinkle with lemon zest, and season with salt and black pepper.
4. Cook for an additional 2-3 minutes, stirring frequently, until the broccoli is evenly coated and heated through. Serve warm.

Grilled Zucchini

 PREPARATION TIME: 5 MINUTES

 COOKING TIME: 10 MINUTES

 SERVES: 4

Nutrition Information (Per Serving):
70 Calories / 5g Fat / 6g Carbohydrates / 1g Protein / 150mg Sodium / 3g Sugar

INGREDIENTS:

- 4 medium zucchinis, sliced lengthwise into 1/4-inch thick strips
- 2 tablespoons olive oil
- 2 cloves fresh garlic, minced
- 1 tablespoon fresh lemon juice
- 1 tablespoon fresh parsley or basil, chopped (for garnish)

*Salt and pepper, to taste

DIRECTIONS:

1. Preheat your grill to medium-high heat.
2. In a large bowl, toss the zucchini slices with olive oil, garlic, salt, and pepper until evenly coated.
3. Place the zucchini slices on the grill and cook for 3-4 minutes on each side, until grill marks appear and the zucchini is tender but not mushy.
4. Remove the zucchini from the grill and drizzle with fresh lemon juice, if desired.
5. Garnish with chopped fresh parsley or basil before serving.

Garlic Roasted Cauliflower

 PREPARATION TIME: 10 MINUTES

 COOKING TIME: 25 MINUTES

 SERVES: 4

Nutrition Information (Per Serving):
120 Calories / 7g Fat / 12g Carbohydrates / 3g Protein / 200mg Sodium / 2g Sugar

INGREDIENTS:

- 1 large head of cauliflower, cut into florets
- 3 cloves garlic, minced
- 3 tablespoons olive oil
- 1 teaspoon smoked paprika
- 1 tablespoon lemon juice

*Salt and pepper to taste
*Fresh parsley, chopped, for garnish (optional)

DIRECTIONS:

1. Preheat your oven to 400°F (200°C).
2. In a large bowl, toss the cauliflower florets with olive oil, minced garlic, smoked paprika, salt, and pepper until evenly coated.
3. Spread the cauliflower in a single layer on a baking sheet lined with parchment paper.
4. Roast in the preheated oven for 20-25 minutes, stirring halfway through, until the cauliflower is tender and golden brown.
5. Remove from the oven and drizzle with lemon juice and garnish with chopped fresh parsley, if desired.

Cucumber Feta Salad

 PREPARATION TIME: 10 MINUTES

 COOKING TIME: NONE

 SERVES: 4

Nutrition Information (Per Serving):
120 Calories / 9g Fat / 7g Carbohydrates / 3g Protein / 350mg Sodium / 3g Sugar

INGREDIENTS:

- 2 large cucumbers, peeled (if preferred) and sliced
- 1/2 cup feta cheese, crumbled
- 1/4 red onion, thinly sliced
- 2 tablespoons extra virgin olive oil
- 1 tablespoon red wine vinegar or lemon juice

*Salt and pepper ,to taste
*Fresh dill chopper for garnish (optional)

DIRECTIONS:

1. In a large bowl, combine the sliced cucumbers and red onion.
2. Add the crumbled feta cheese to the bowl.
3. Drizzle the olive oil and red wine vinegar or lemon juice over the salad.
4. Add the chopped fresh dill, if using, and season with salt and pepper.
5. Toss gently to combine all ingredients.
6. Serve immediately or chill in the refrigerator for a more refreshing taste.

Arugula and Parmesan Salad

 PREPARATION TIME: 5 MINUTES

 COOKING TIME: NONE

SERVES: 4

Nutrition Information (Per Serving):
110 Calories / 9g Fat / 4g Carbohydrates / 4g Protein / 220mg Sodium / 1g Sugar

INGREDIENTS:

- 4 cups fresh arugula leaves
- 1/4 cup shaved Parmesan cheese
- 2 tablespoons extra virgin olive oil
- 1 tablespoon lemon juice
- 1/4 cup toasted pine nuts or walnuts (optional)

*Salt and pepper to taste

DIRECTIONS:

1. Place the arugula leaves in a large salad bowl.
2. Drizzle the olive oil and lemon juice over the arugula.
3. Toss the salad gently to coat the arugula evenly with the dressing.
4. Sprinkle the shaved Parmesan cheese over the salad.
5. Season with salt and pepper to taste.
6. Add toasted pine nuts or walnuts for extra texture and flavor, if using.
7. Serve immediately as a light and refreshing side dish.

Turkish Green Beans with Almonds

PREPARATION TIME: 10 MINUTES

COOKING TIME: 15-10 MINUTES

SERVES: 4

Nutrition Information (Per Serving):
130 Calories / 8g Fat / 12g Carbohydrates / 3g Protein /
200mg Sodium / 3g Sugar

INGREDIENTS:

- 1 pound green beans, trimmed
- 2 tablespoons olive oil
- 2 cloves garlic, minced
- 1/4 cup sliced almonds, toasted
- 1 lemon, juiced

*Salt and pepper, to taste

DIRECTIONS:

1. In a large skillet, heat the olive oil over medium heat. Add the minced garlic and sauté for 1-2 minutes until fragrant.
2. Add the green beans to the skillet and stir well to coat them in the garlic and olive oil. Cook for about 10-15 minutes, stirring occasionally, until the beans are tender-crisp.
3. Drizzle the lemon juice over the green beans and stir to combine.
4. Sprinkle the toasted almonds over the green beans and stir gently to mix.
5. Season with salt and pepper to taste, and serve hot as a delicious Mediterranean dish.

Spanakorizo (Spinach Rice)

PREPARATION TIME: 10 MINUTES

COOKING TIME: 25 MINUTES

SERVES: 4

Nutrition Information (Per Serving):
180 Calories / 7g Fat / 28g Carbohydrates / 4g Protein /
300mg Sodium / 2g Sugar

INGREDIENTS:

- 1 cup white rice (uncooked)
- 4 cups fresh spinach, chopped
- 1 onion, finely chopped
- 2 tablespoons olive oil
- 1 lemon, juiced

*Salt and pepper, to taste

DIRECTIONS:

1. In a large skillet, heat the olive oil over medium heat. Add the chopped onion and sauté for 3-4 minutes until soft and translucent.
2. Stir in the uncooked rice and cook for 1-2 minutes, allowing it to be coated with the oil and onion mixture.
3. Add 2 cups of water to the skillet and bring to a boil. Reduce the heat to low, cover, and let it simmer for about 15 minutes, or until the rice is nearly cooked.
4. Stir in the chopped spinach and lemon juice. Cover again and cook for another 5-7 minutes, or until the spinach is wilted and the rice is fully cooked.
5. Fluff the rice with a fork, season with salt and pepper to taste, and serve warm.

Farro with Mushrooms and Carrots

 PREPARATION TIME: 10 MINUTES

 COOKING TIME: 25-30 MINUTES

 SERVES: 4

Nutrition Information (Per Serving):
220 Calories / 9g Fat / 32g Carbohydrates / 7g Protein / 150mg Sodium / 2g Sugar

INGREDIENTS:

- 1 cup farro, rinsed
- 2 cups mushrooms, sliced
- 2 medium carrots, diced
- 2 tablespoons olive oil
- 1 onion, finely chopped

*Salt and pepper, to taste

DIRECTIONS:

1. In a medium pot, cook the farro according to package instructions until tender, about 20-25 minutes. Drain and set aside.
2. In a large skillet, heat the olive oil over medium heat. Add the chopped onion and sauté for 3-4 minutes until it becomes soft and translucent.
3. Stir in the sliced mushrooms and diced carrots. Cook for an additional 8-10 minutes, stirring occasionally, until the vegetables are tender.
4. Add the cooked farro to the skillet with the vegetables. Stir well to combine and season with salt and pepper to taste.
5. Serve warm as a hearty side dish.

Caramelized Onions and Peppers

 PREPARATION TIME: 10 MINUTES

 COOKING TIME: 30 MINUTES

 SERVES: 4

Nutrition Information (Per Serving):
150 Calories / 7g Fat / 20g Carbohydrates / 2g Protein / 200mg Sodium / 8g Sugar

INGREDIENTS:

- 2 large onions, thinly sliced
- 2 large bell peppers (any color), thinly sliced
- 2 tablespoons olive oil
- 1 tablespoon balsamic vinegar (optional)
- 1 teaspoon sugar (optional, for extra caramelization)

*Salt and pepper to taste
*Fresh thyme or basil for garnish (optional)

DIRECTIONS:

1. In a large skillet, heat the olive oil over medium heat.
2. Add the sliced onions to the skillet and cook, stirring occasionally, for about 10 minutes until the onions begin to soften and turn golden.
3. Add the sliced bell peppers to the skillet. Continue to cook, stirring occasionally, for another 15-20 minutes, until both the onions and peppers are deeply caramelized and tender.
4. If desired, stir in the balsamic vinegar and sugar for extra depth of flavor and enhanced caramelization. Cook for an additional 2-3 minutes.
5. Season with salt and pepper to taste.
6. Garnish with fresh thyme or basil if desired, and serve warm.

Chapter ⑥

Desserts

Lemon Olive Oil Cake

 PREPARATION TIME: 15 MINUTES

 COOKING TIME: 30-40 MINUTES

 SERVES: 8-10

Nutrition Information (Per Serving):
260 Calories / 12g Fat / 34g Carbohydrates / 4g Protein / 140mg Sodium / 18g Sugar

INGREDIENTS:

- 1 1/2 cups all-purpose flour
- 1 cup sugar
- 3 large eggs
- 1/2 cup olive oil
- 1 lemon, zested and juiced

*Pinch of salt, to test
*Dust with powdered sugar for garnish (optional)

DIRECTIONS:

1. Preheat your oven to 350°F (175°C). Grease a 9-inch round cake pan or line it with parchment paper.
2. In a large bowl, whisk together the eggs, olive oil, lemon zest, and lemon juice until well combined.
3. Gradually add the flour, sugar, and a pinch of salt to the wet ingredients, stirring until the batter is smooth and free of lumps.
4. Pour the batter into the prepared cake pan and smooth the top. Bake in the preheated oven for 35-40 minutes, or until a toothpick inserted into the center of the cake comes out clean.
5. Allow the cake to cool in the pan for 10 minutes before transferring it to a wire rack to cool completely. Dust with powdered sugar if desired.

Honey Ricotta with Fresh Berries

 PREPARATION TIME: 10 MINUTES

 COOKING TIME: 10 MINUTES

 SERVES: 4

Nutrition Information (Per Serving):
220 Calories / 12g Fat / 19g Carbohydrates / 8g Protein / 80mg Sodium / 16g Sugar

INGREDIENTS:

- 1 cup ricotta cheese
- 2 tablespoons honey
- 1 cup mixed fresh berries (such as strawberries, blueberries, and raspberries)
- 1/4 teaspoon vanilla extract (optional)
- Mint leaves for garnish (optional)

DIRECTIONS:

1. In a medium bowl, mix the ricotta cheese with honey and vanilla extract (if using) until smooth and creamy.
2. Divide the ricotta mixture evenly into serving bowls.
3. Top each bowl with the mixed fresh berries.
4. Garnish with a few mint leaves if desired and serve immediately.
5. Serve immediately.

TIP: For an added crunch and flavor boost, sprinkle some chopped almonds or walnuts over the berries before serving!

Honey Almond Cookies

⚒ **PREPARATION TIME:** 15 MINUTES

⏱ **COOKING TIME:** 12-15 MINUTES

👥 **SERVES:** 12 COOKIES

Nutrition Information (Per Cookie):
120 Calories / 7g Fat / 12g Carbohydrates / 2g Protein /
50mg Sodium / 8g Sugar

INGREDIENTS:

- 1 cup almond flour
- 1/4 cup honey
- 1/4 cup butter, melted
- 1/2 teaspoon vanilla extract
- 1/4 teaspoon baking powder

*Pinch of salt (optional)

*Sliced almonds for decoration (optional)

DIRECTIONS:

1. Preheat your oven to 350°F (175°C). Line a baking sheet with parchment paper.
2. In a large bowl, mix together the almond flour, honey, melted butter, vanilla extract, baking powder, and a pinch of salt (if using) until a smooth dough forms.
3. Scoop small portions of the dough and roll them into balls. Place the balls on the prepared baking sheet and gently flatten each one with your hand or the back of a spoon.
4. If desired, press a few sliced almonds into the top of each cookie. Bake in the preheated oven for 12-15 minutes, or until the edges are golden brown.
5. Allow the cookies to cool on the baking sheet for a few minutes before transferring them to a wire rack to cool completely.

Fig and Honey Tart

⚒ **PREPARATION TIME:** 20 MINUTES

⏱ **COOKING TIME:** 25-30 MINUTES

👥 **SERVES:** 6-8

Nutrition Information (Per Serving):
260 Calories / 14g Fat / 30g Carbohydrates / 4g Protein /
120mg Sodium / 15g Sugar

INGREDIENTS:

- 1 sheet puff pastry, thawed
- 8-10 fresh figs, sliced
- 1/4 cup honey
- 1/4 cup ricotta cheese (or cream cheese)
- Chopped walnuts (optional, for added crunch)

*Pinch of salt (optional)

DIRECTIONS:

1. Preheat your oven to 400°F (200°C). Line a baking sheet with parchment paper.
2. Place the puff pastry sheet on the prepared baking sheet. Spread a thin layer of ricotta cheese (or cream cheese) over the surface, leaving a small border around the edges.
3. Layer the fig slices evenly on top of the ricotta cheese, slightly overlapping them.
4. Drizzle the honey evenly over the figs and sprinkle with a pinch of salt if desired.
5. Bake in the preheated oven for 20-25 minutes, or until the pastry is golden brown and puffed.
6. Allow the tart to cool slightly before serving. Garnish with chopped walnuts for an extra crunch, if desired.

Chocolate-Dipped Apricots

PREPARATION TIME: 10 MINUTES

COOKING TIME: 15-20 MINUTES

CHILLING TIME: 15-20 MINUTES

SERVES: 24 pieces

Nutrition Information (per piece):
60 Calories / 3g Fat / 7g Carbohydrates / 1g Protein / 10mg Sodium / 6g Sugar

INGREDIENTS:

- 24 dried apricots
- 1 cup dark chocolate chips (or chocolate bar, chopped)
- 1 tablespoon coconut oil
- Sea salt (optional, for a touch of flavor)

DIRECTIONS:

1. In a microwave-safe bowl, combine the dark chocolate chips and coconut oil. Microwave in 30-second intervals, stirring in between, until the chocolate is fully melted and smooth.
2. Dip each dried apricot halfway into the melted chocolate, allowing the excess to drip off. Place the dipped apricots on a parchment-lined baking sheet.
3. Sprinkle the chocolate-dipped apricots with a light sprinkle of sea salt, if desired.
4. Let the apricots cool at room temperature or place them in the refrigerator for 15-20 minutes until the chocolate is set.
5. Enjoy the chocolate-dipped apricots as a sweet snack or dessert.

Lemon Ricotta Cheesecake

PREPARATION TIME: 15 MINUTES

COOKING TIME: 50-55 MINUTES

CHILLING TIME: 2 HOURS

SERVES: 6-8

Nutrition Information (Per Serving): 260 Calories/14g Fat/22g Carbohydrates/12g Protein/160mg Sodium/18g Sugar

INGREDIENTS:

- 2 cups ricotta cheese
- 3/4 cup granulated sugar
- 3 large eggs
- Zest and juice of 1 lemon
- 1 cup crushed graham crackers or biscuits (optional for crust, or omit for crustless cheesecake)

DIRECTIONS:

1. Preheat your oven to 350°F (180°C) and, if using, lightly grease a 9-inch springform pan and press the crushed graham crackers into the base.
2. In a large mixing bowl, beat together the ricotta cheese and sugar until smooth and creamy.
3. Add the eggs one at a time, mixing well after each addition.
4. Stir in the lemon zest and juice, blending thoroughly.
5. Pour the mixture into the prepared pan, spreading evenly over the crust if using.
6. Bake for 50-60 minutes or until the cheesecake is set and the edges are lightly golden.
7. Allow the cheesecake to cool completely, then refrigerate for at least 2 hours before serving.

Honey and Cinnamon Baked Grapefruit

PREPARATION TIME: 5 MINUTES

COOKING TIME: 10 - 12 MINUTES

SERVES: 4

Nutrition Information (Per Serving):
90 Calories / 2g Fat / 20g Carbohydrates / 1g Protein / 0mg Sodium / 18g Sugar

INGREDIENTS:

- 2 large grapefruits
- 4 tablespoons honey
- 1 teaspoon ground cinnamon
- 1/2 teaspoon vanilla extract (optional)
- Fresh mint or thyme for garnish (optional)

DIRECTIONS:

1. Preheat the oven to 375°F (190°C). Line a baking sheet with parchment paper.
2. Cut the grapefruits in half and use a small knife to loosen the segments for easier eating.
3. Place the grapefruit halves on the prepared baking sheet.
4. Drizzle each grapefruit half with honey and sprinkle with ground cinnamon. Add a few drops of vanilla extract if using.
5. Bake in the preheated oven for 10 - 12 minutes, or until the tops are slightly caramelized.
6. Remove from the oven and let cool for a few minutes. Garnish with fresh mint leaves or thyme, if desired and serve warm.

Pomegranate and Nuts Frozen Yogurt Slice

PREPARATION TIME: 15 MINUTES

COOKING TIME: NIONE

FREEZING TIME: 3-4 HOURS

SERVES: 6-8

Nutrition Information (Per Serving):
160 Calories / 6g Fat / 18g Carbohydrates / 8g Protein / 30mg Sodium / 12g Sugar

INGREDIENTS:

- 2 cups Greek yogurt
- 1/4 cup honey
- 1/2 cup pomegranate seeds
- 1/4 cup chopped nuts (such as almonds, pistachios, or walnuts)
- 1/2 teaspoon vanilla extract (optional)

DIRECTIONS:

1. In a large bowl, combine the Greek yogurt, honey, and vanilla extract (if using). Stir until smooth and well blended.
2. Gently fold in the pomegranate seeds and chopped nuts, reserving a few for garnish.
3. Line a small baking dish or loaf pan with parchment paper. Spread the yogurt mixture evenly into the pan.
4. Sprinkle the remaining pomegranate seeds and nuts over the top, pressing them slightly into the yogurt.
5. Place the pan in the freezer for 3-4 hours, or until the yogurt is firm and set.
6. Once frozen, lift the yogurt out of the pan using the parchment paper, slice it into pieces, and serve immediately.

Grapes in Muscat Syrup

PREPARATION TIME: 5 MINUTES

COOKING TIME: NONE

CHILLING TIME: 1 HOUR

SERVES: 4

Nutrition Information (Per Serving):
120 Calories / 0g Fat / 28g Carbohydrates / 1g Protein / 0mg Sodium / 26g Sugar

INGREDIENTS:

- 2 cups seedless grapes (red or green)
- 1/2 cup Muscat wine (or any sweet dessert wine)
- 2 tablespoons honey
- 1 teaspoon lemon juice
- 1/2 teaspoon vanilla extract

*Fresh mint leaves for garnish (optional)

DIRECTIONS:

1. In a small saucepan, combine the Muscat wine, honey, lemon juice, and vanilla extract.
2. Bring the mixture to a gentle simmer over low heat, stirring until the honey is fully dissolved.
3. Remove from heat and let the syrup cool to room temperature.
4. Place the grapes in a serving bowl or divide them into individual dessert glasses.
5. Pour the cooled syrup over the grapes, making sure they are well coated.
6. Cover and refrigerate for at least 1 hour to allow the flavors to meld.
7. Serve the chilled grapes in their syrup, garnished with fresh mint leaves if desired.

Mahalabia (Middle Eastern Milk Pudding)

PREPARATION TIME: 10 MINUTES

COOKING TIME: 10 MINUTES

CHILLING TIME: 1-2 HOURS

SERVES: 4

Nutrition Information (Per Serving):
150 Calories / 5g Fat / 22g Carbohydrates / 4g Protein / 45mg Sodium / 15g Sugar

INGREDIENTS:

- 2 cups whole milk
- 1/4 cup sugar
- 2 tablespoons cornstarch
- 1 teaspoon rosewater (or orange blossom water)

*Crushed pistachios (optional, for garnish)

DIRECTIONS:

1. In a saucepan, heat the milk over medium heat. Add the sugar and stir until it dissolves.
2. In a small bowl, dissolve the cornstarch in a little bit of cold water to make a smooth paste. Slowly pour the cornstarch mixture into the milk, stirring constantly.
3. Continue to cook and stir the milk mixture over medium heat until it thickens to a pudding-like consistency, about 5-7 minutes.
4. Remove the saucepan from the heat and stir in the rosewater (or orange blossom water).
5. Pour the pudding into serving bowls and let it cool to room temperature. Then, refrigerate for 1-2 hours until it sets completely.
6. Before serving, sprinkle with crushed pistachios if desired.

Yogurt and Berry Parfait

PREPARATION TIME: 10 MINUTES

COOKING TIME: 10 MINUTES

SERVES: 4

Nutrition Information (Per Serving):
180 Calories / 6g Fat / 25g Carbohydrates / 7g Protein / 70mg Sodium / 18g Sugar

INGREDIENTS:

- 2 cups Greek yogurt
- 2 tablespoons honey or maple syrup
- 1 teaspoon vanilla extract
- 2 cups mixed berries (strawberries, blueberries, raspberries)
- 1/2 cup granola

*Fresh mint leaves for garnish (optional)

DIRECTIONS:

1. In a medium bowl, stir together the Greek yogurt, honey, and vanilla extract until smooth and well combined. Taste and adjust the sweetness by adding more honey if desired.
2. Spoon a layer of the yogurt mixture into the bottom of each serving glass or bowl.
3. Top the yogurt with a layer of mixed berries, followed by a sprinkle of granola.
4. Add another layer of yogurt, then more berries and granola.
5. Continue layering until the glasses are full, finishing with berries and a sprinkle of granola on top.
6. Garnish each parfait with fresh mint leaves if desired.

Panna Cotta with Honey

PREPARATION TIME: 10 MINUTES

COOKING TIME: 10 MINUTES

CHILLING TIME: 4 HOURS

SERVES: 4-6

Nutrition Information (Per Serving):
240 Calories / 18g Fat / 18g Carbohydrates / 3g Protein / 40mg Sodium / 15g Sugar

INGREDIENTS:

- 2 cups heavy cream
- 1/4 cup honey
- 1 teaspoon vanilla extract
- 2 teaspoons gelatin powder
- 2 tablespoons cold water

DIRECTIONS:

1. In a small bowl, sprinkle the gelatin powder over the cold water and let it sit for 5 minutes to bloom.
2. In a saucepan, heat the heavy cream, honey, and vanilla extract over medium heat until it's just about to boil. Stir occasionally to dissolve the honey.
3. Remove the saucepan from the heat and stir in the bloomed gelatin until it completely dissolves into the cream mixture.
4. Pour the mixture into individual serving molds or ramekins.
5. Refrigerate for at least 4 hours or until the panna cotta is firm and set.
6. To serve, unmold the panna cotta onto a plate or enjoy directly from the ramekins. Drizzle with a little extra honey if desired.

Pomegranate Sorbet

🍴 **PREPARATION TIME:** 10 MINUTES

🕐 **COOKING TIME:** NONE

❄️ **CHILLING TIME:** 3-4 HOURS

👥 **SERVES:** 4-6

Nutrition Information (Per Serving):
120 Calories / 0g Fat / 28g Carbohydrates / 1g Protein / 0mg Sodium / 26g Sugar

INGREDIENTS:

- 2 cups pomegranate juice
- 1/2 cup sugar
- 1/4 cup water
- 1 tablespoon lemon juice
- Pomegranate seeds (optional, for garnish)

DIRECTIONS:

1. In a small saucepan, combine the sugar and water. Heat over medium heat, stirring until the sugar is completely dissolved. Let it cool to room temperature.
2. In a bowl, mix the pomegranate juice, lemon juice, and the cooled simple syrup.
3. Pour the mixture into a shallow container and place it in the freezer. Stir the sorbet every 30 minutes for the first 2 hours to break up any ice crystals.
4. Let the sorbet freeze for an additional 2 hours, or until it is firm and scoopable.
5. Scoop the pomegranate sorbet into bowls and garnish with pomegranate seeds, if desired.

Pasteli (Sesame Bars)

🍴 **PREPARATION TIME:** 5 MINUTES

🕐 **COOKING TIME:** 15 MINUTES

❄️ **COOLING TIME:** 1 HOUR

👥 **SERVES:** 8-10

Nutrition Information (Per Serving):
180 Calories / 10g Fat / 18g Carbohydrates / 4g Protein / 10mg Sodium / 12g Sugar

INGREDIENTS:

- 1 cup sesame seeds
- 1/2 cup honey
- 1/4 cup chopped nuts of your choice (walnuts, pistachios, almonds)
- 1/2 teaspoon lemon zest
- 1/2 teaspoon cinnamon (optional, for added warmth and spice)

DIRECTIONS:

1. In a dry skillet, lightly toast the sesame seeds over medium heat for 3-4 minutes, stirring frequently until golden and fragrant. Remove from heat and set aside.
2. In a saucepan, heat the honey over medium heat until it starts to bubble. Stir in the lemon zest and let it simmer for 2-3 minutes.
3. Add the toasted sesame seeds and chopped nuts to the saucepan with the honey. Stir well until all the ingredients are evenly coated.
4. Pour the mixture onto a parchment-lined baking sheet and press it into an even layer using a spatula or the back of a spoon.
5. Let the mixture cool at room temperature for about 1 hour, or until it hardens. Once set, cut it into bars or squares.
6. Enjoy these Nutty Sesame Bars as a sweet, energy-boosting snack or dessert.

Orange and Almond Cake

PREPARATION TIME: 15 MINUTES

COOKING TIME: 1 AND 1/2 HOURS

SERVES: 6-8

Nutrition Information (Per Serving):
240 Calories / 12g Fat / 28g Carbohydrates / 6g Protein / 80mg Sodium / 18g Sugar

INGREDIENTS:

- 2 large oranges, whole
- 4 eggs
- 1 cup almond flour
- 1/2 cup honey
- 1 teaspoon baking powder

DIRECTIONS:

1. Preheat your oven to 350°F (175°C). Grease a 9-inch round cake pan and line it with parchment paper.
2. In a saucepan, boil the whole oranges (with the peel on) for about 15-20 minutes until they are soft. Allow them to cool, then cut into pieces and remove any seeds.
3. In a blender or food processor, blend the boiled oranges until you have a smooth puree.
4. In a large bowl, whisk together the eggs, honey, almond flour, and baking powder. Stir in the orange puree until well combined.
5. Pour the batter into the prepared cake pan and bake for 40-45 minutes, or until a toothpick inserted into the center comes out clean.
6. Allow the cake to cool in the pan for 10 minutes before transferring it to a wire rack to cool completely.

Stuffed Dates with Nuts and Goat Cheese

PREPARATION TIME: 15 MINUTES

COOKING TIME: 15 MINUTES

SERVES: 8-10

Nutrition Information (Per Serving):
120 Calories / 6g Fat / 14g Carbohydrates / 3g Protein / 60mg Sodium / 11g Sugar

INGREDIENTS:

- 20 Medjool dates, pitted
- 4 oz goat cheese, softened
- 1/4 cup chopped nuts (such as almonds, walnuts, or pistachios)
- 1 tablespoon honey (optional, for drizzling)
- Fresh herbs (such as thyme or rosemary) for garnish (optional)

DIRECTIONS:

1. Slice each date lengthwise to create an opening, being careful not to cut all the way through.
2. Fill each date with about 1/2 teaspoon of goat cheese.
3. Sprinkle the stuffed dates with chopped nuts.
4. Arrange the dates on a serving platter.
5. If desired, drizzle with honey and garnish with fresh herbs.
6. Serve immediately.

TIP: For added flavor, lightly toast the nuts before using them to fill the dates.

Baked Pears with Honey

⚒ **PREPARATION TIME:** 10 MINUTES

🕐 **COOKING TIME:** 20-25 MINUTES

👥 **SERVES:** 4

Nutrition Information (Per Serving):
180 Calories / 7g Fat / 28g Carbohydrates / 2g Protein /
15mg Sodium / 18g Sugar

INGREDIENTS:

- 4 ripe pears, halved and cored
- 2 tablespoons honey
- 1 teaspoon cinnamon
- 1/4 cup walnuts and raisin, chopped (optional, for garnish)
- 1 tablespoon butter, melted

DIRECTIONS:

1. Preheat your oven to 375°F (190°C). Line a baking dish with parchment paper or lightly grease it.
2. Arrange the halved and cored pears in the baking dish with the cut side facing up.
3. Drizzle each pear half with honey, sprinkle with cinnamon, and brush lightly with the melted butter.
4. Bake in the preheated oven for 20-25 minutes, or until the pears are tender and slightly caramelized.
5. Garnish the baked pears with chopped walnuts if desired, and serve warm.

Baklava Bites

⚒ **PREPARATION TIME:** 15 MINUTES

🕐 **COOKING TIME:** 20-25 MINUTES

👥 **SERVES:** 6

Nutrition Information (Per Serving):
130 Calories / 9g Fat / 12g Carbohydrates / 2g Protein /
50mg Sodium / 8g Sugar

INGREDIENTS:

- 1 sheet phyllo dough, thawed
- 1/2 cup chopped nuts (such as almonds, walnuts, or pistachios)
- 1/4 cup honey
- 1/4 cup butter, melted
- 1/2 teaspoon cinnamon

DIRECTIONS:

1. Preheat your oven to 350°F (175°C). Grease a mini muffin tin or line it with paper liners.
2. Cut the phyllo dough into small squares that fit into the mini muffin tin cups. Layer 3-4 squares of phyllo in each cup, brushing each layer lightly with melted butter.
3. In a bowl, mix the chopped nuts with cinnamon. Spoon a small amount of the nut mixture into each phyllo cup.
4. Drizzle a little honey over each filled cup. Bake in the preheated oven for 20-25 minutes, or until the phyllo is golden brown and crispy.
5. Allow the baklava bites to cool slightly before removing them from the muffin tin. Drizzle with additional honey if desired and serve.

Almond Nougat

 PREPARATION TIME: 10 MINUTES

 COOKING TIME: 20-25 MINUTES

 SERVES: 10-12 PIECES

Nutrition Information (Per piece):
130 Calories / 5g Fat / 19g Carbohydrates / 2g Protein /
40mg Sodium / 16g Sugar

INGREDIENTS:

- 1 cup whole almonds, toasted
- 1 cup granulated sugar
- 1/2 cup honey
- 2 large egg whites
- 1/4 teaspoon salt

DIRECTIONS:

1. Toast the almonds in a dry skillet over medium heat for 5-7 minutes until golden and fragrant. Set aside to cool.
2. In a saucepan, heat the sugar and honey over medium heat until the mixture reaches 140°C (285°F) on a candy thermometer, then reduce to a simmer.
3. While the sugar mixture is heating, beat the egg whites and salt in a separate bowl until stiff peaks form.
4. Slowly pour the hot sugar syrup into the egg whites while continuously beating on low speed until fully combined and the mixture thickens.
5. Fold in the toasted almonds, then transfer the nougat mixture to a parchment-lined pan, spreading it evenly to a thickness of 1/2 to 3/4 inch.
6. Allow the nougat to cool completely, then cut it into pieces and enjoy.

Rosewater Saffron Rice Pudding

 PREPARATION TIME: 5 MINUTES

 COOKING TIME: 30-35 MINUTES

 SERVES: 4

Nutrition Information (Per Serving):
210 Calories / 5g Fat / 38g Carbohydrates / 6g Protein /
80mg Sodium / 20g Sugar

INGREDIENTS:

- 1/2 cup basmati rice
- 4 cups whole milk
- 1/2 cup granulated sugar
- 1/4 teaspoon saffron threads
- 1 tablespoon rosewater

Decorations (optional):
-Crushed pistachios
-Edible rose petals
-A sprinkle of ground cardamom

DIRECTIONS:

1. Rinse the basmati rice thoroughly and drain.
2. In a medium saucepan, bring the milk to a gentle boil over medium heat. Add the rice and reduce the heat to low.
3. Cook the rice in the milk, stirring occasionally, for about 25-30 minutes or until the rice is tender and the mixture thickens.
4. Stir in the sugar, saffron threads, and rosewater. Continue to cook for an additional 5 minutes, stirring continuously, until the sugar dissolves and the flavors blend.
5. Remove from heat and let the pudding cool slightly. Serve warm or chilled, garnished with a few saffron threads if desired.

TIP: Soak saffron threads in warm milk before adding for enhanced color and aroma.

Chapter

Refreshers

Lemon Mint Cooler

PREPARATION TIME: 10 MINUTES

COOKING TIME: NONE

CHILLING TIME: 20-30 MINUTES

SERVES: 6-8 GLASSES

Nutrition Information (Per Serving):
50 Calories / 0g Fat / 13g Carbohydrates / 0g Protein / 4mg Sodium / 12g Sugar

INGREDIENTS:

- 3/4 cup fresh lemon juice (about 4-6 lemons)
- 1/3 cup fresh mint leaves
- 1/3 cup sugar (adjust to taste)
- 6 cups cold water
- Ice cubes (as needed)

DIRECTIONS:

1. In a large pitcher or jar, mix the fresh lemon juice and sugar, stirring until the sugar dissolves completely.
2. Add the fresh mint leaves and gently muddle them to release their flavor.
3. Pour in the cold water and stir well to combine.
4. Add ice cubes and chill in the refrigerator for at least 20-30 minutes before serving.
5. Serve in individual glasses with extra ice and a sprig of mint for garnish.

TIP: Add lemon slices and crushed mint to the pitcher for extra flavor.

Traditional Hot Turkish Tea with Lemon

PREPARATION TIME: 10 MINUTES

COOKING TIME: NONE

BREWING TIME: 15-20 MINUTES

SERVES: 4 CUPS

Nutrition Information (Per Cup):
5 Calories / 0g Fat / 1g Carbohydrates / 0g Protein / 0mg Sodium / 1g Sugar (without added sugar)

INGREDIENTS:

- 4 cups of brewed black tea (strong)
- Juice of 1 lemon
- 3 tablespoons honey (adjust to taste)
- 1/2 lemon, sliced

DIRECTIONS:

1. In a medium saucepan, boil 4 cups of water.
2. Add 3 tablespoons of loose black tea leaves to a small teapot.
3. Pour 1 cup of boiling water into the teapot to bloom the tea leaves.
4. Add the remaining water to the teapot, then place it on the saucepan and let it simmer for 15-20 minutes.
5. After simmering, pour the concentrated tea into each Turkish tea glass or regular cup.
6. Add the juice of 1 lemon and a lemon slice to each glass.
7. Dilute with hot water to your desired strength.
8. Serve with sugar on the side for individual taste.

Iced Greek Frappe

![whisk icon] **PREPARATION TIME:** 10 MINUTES

![clock icon] **COOKING TIME:** NONE

![serves icon] **SERVES:** 4 GLASSES

Nutrition Information (Per Glass):
40 Calories / 0g Fat / 9g Carbohydrates / 1g Protein / 10mg Sodium / 8g Sugar

INGREDIENTS:

- 1/3 cup instant coffee
- 1 cup cold water
- 1/4 cup sugar (optional, adjust to taste)
- 1 cup milk (optional)
- Ice cubes (as needed)

DIRECTIONS:

1. In a shaker or blender, combine the instant coffee, cold water, and sugar.
2. Blend or shake vigorously for about 20-30 seconds, or until a thick foam forms.
3. Pour the coffee mixture into a pitcher filled with ice cubes.
4. Add milk to taste, or leave it black for a stronger coffee flavor.
5. Stir well before serving, and pour into individual glasses filled with ice if desired.

TIP: For an even creamier texture, blend the frappe with a small scoop of vanilla ice cream or a splash of evaporated milk before serving.

Pomegranate Spritzer

![whisk icon] **PREPARATION TIME:** 5 MINUTES

![clock icon] **COOKING TIME:** NONE

![serves icon] **SERVES:** 6-8 GLASSES

Nutrition Information (Per Serving):
50 Calories / 0g Fat / 13g Carbohydrates / 0g Protein / 5mg Sodium / 12g Sugar

INGREDIENTS:

- 3 cups pomegranate juice
- 3 cups sparkling water
- Juice of 1 1/2 limes
- Ice cubes (as needed)
- Fresh rosemary for garnish (optional)

DIRECTIONS:

1. In a large pitcher, combine the pomegranate juice and lime juice.
2. Add the sparkling water and stir gently to mix.
3. Fill each glass with ice cubes, then pour the pomegranate mixture over the ice.
4. Garnish each glass with fresh rosemary for a refreshing finish, if desired.
5. Serve immediately to enjoy its bubbly, tart flavor.

TIP: For a touch of elegance, add a few pomegranate seeds to each glass before serving to enhance the flavor and appearance.

Rosewater Lemonade

 PREPARATION TIME: 10 MINUTES

 COOKING TIME: NONE

SERVES: 6-8 GLASSES

Nutrition Information (Per Glass):
60 Calories / 0g Fat / 16g Carbohydrates / 0g Protein / 5mg Sodium / 15g Sugar

INGREDIENTS:

- 1 1/2 cups fresh lemon juice (about 8-10 lemons)
- 1/2 cup sugar (adjust to taste)
- 8 cups cold water
- 2 tablespoons rosewater
- Ice cubes (as needed)

*Lemon slices and fresh mint leaves for garnish (optional)

DIRECTIONS:

1. In a large pitcher, combine the fresh lemon juice and sugar, stirring until the sugar is fully dissolved.
2. Add the rosewater and cold water, then stir well to blend all the ingredients.
3. Fill each glass with ice cubes, and pour the rosewater lemonade mixture over the ice.
4. Garnish with lemon slices and fresh mint leaves for an extra touch of flavor and color.
5. Serve immediately for a refreshing, aromatic drink.

Minty Yogurt Lassi

 PREPARATION TIME: 5 MINUTES

COOKING TIME: NONE

SERVES: 4 GLASSES

Nutrition Information (Per Serving):
90 Calories / 3g Fat / 9g Carbohydrates / 6g Protein / 150mg Sodium / 6g Sugar

INGREDIENTS:

- 2 cups Greek yogurt
- 1 cup cold water
- 1/4 cup fresh mint leaves
- 1/2 teaspoon salt
- Ice cubes (as needed)

DIRECTIONS:

1. In a blender, combine the Greek yogurt, cold water, fresh mint leaves, and salt.
2. Blend until the mixture is smooth and frothy.
3. Fill each glass with ice cubes, then pour the lassi over the ice.
4. Garnish with a few mint leaves on top for extra freshness.
5. Serve immediately and enjoy the cool, refreshing taste.

TIP: For an extra burst of flavor, chill the mint leaves before blending to enhance the minty freshness in your lassi.

Ayran
(Cucumber Yogurt Drink)

⚒ **PREPARATION TIME:** 5 MINUTES

⏱ **COOKING TIME:** NONE

👥 **SERVES:** 6 - 8 GLASSES

Nutrition Information (Per Glass):
70 Calories / 2g Fat / 6g Carbohydrates / 5g Protein / 200mg Sodium / 5g Sugar

INGREDIENTS:

- 2 cups Greek yogurt
- 1 cup cold water
- 1 small cucumber, finely grated or chopped
- 1/2 teaspoon salt
- Ice cubes (as needed)

*Mint leaves for garnish (optional)

DIRECTIONS:

1. In a blender, combine the Greek yogurt, cold water, and salt.
2. Add the grated cucumber and blend until smooth and well combined.
3. Fill each glass with ice cubes, then pour the Ayran over the ice.
4. Stir well and serve immediately, garnished with a few fresh mint leaves if desired.

TIP: Chill the yogurt and cucumber in the refrigerator before blending to make your Ayran extra cold and refreshing.

Fig and Honey
Iced Tea

⚒ **PREPARATION TIME:** 5 MINUTES

⏱ **COOKING TIME:** NONE

❄ **CHILLING TIME:** 30 MINUTES

👥 **SERVES:** 4 GLASSES

Nutrition Information (Per Serving): 60 Calories/0g Fat/16g Carbohydrates/0g Protein/5mg Sodium/15g Sugar

INGREDIENTS:

- 4 cups water
- 4 black tea bags
- 4 fresh figs, sliced
- 3 tablespoons honey (adjust to taste)
- Ice cubes (as needed)

DIRECTIONS:

1. Boil the water in a saucepan, then remove from heat and add the black tea bags. Let them steep for about 5 minutes.
2. Remove the tea bags and stir in the honey until fully dissolved.
3. Add the sliced figs to the warm tea and let it cool to room temperature.
4. Once cooled, place the tea in the refrigerator to chill for at least 30 minutes.
5. Fill each glass with ice cubes, then pour the fig-infused tea over the ice.
6. Garnish with additional fig slices or a sprig of mint for extra flavor.

TIP: For a stronger fig flavor, gently muddle the figs in the tea before chilling to release more of their natural sweetness.

Watermelon Basil Cooler

⚔ **PREPARATION TIME:** 10 MINUTES

⏱ **COOKING TIME:** NONE

👥 **SERVES:** 4 GLASSES

Nutrition Information (Per Glass):
50 Calories / 0g Fat / 12g Carbohydrates / 1g Protein / 5mg Sodium / 10g Sugar

INGREDIENTS:

- 4 cups fresh watermelon juice (blended watermelon)
- 1/4 cup fresh basil leaves
- Juice of 1 lime
- 1 cup sparkling water
- Ice cubes (as needed)

DIRECTIONS:

1. In a blender, blend the watermelon pieces until smooth. Strain the juice if desired to remove the pulp.
2. In a large pitcher, combine the watermelon juice, lime juice, and fresh basil leaves.
3. Gently muddle the basil leaves with a spoon to release their aroma and flavor.
4. Add the sparkling water and stir well.
5. Fill each glass with ice cubes and pour the Watermelon Basil Cooler over the ice.
6. Garnish with a basil leaf or a small slice of watermelon on the rim.

Limoncello Spritz

⚔ **PREPARATION TIME:** 5 MINUTES

⏱ **COOKING TIME:** NONE

👥 **SERVES:** 4 GLASSES

Nutrition Information (Per Serving):
120 Calories / 0g Fat / 14g Carbohydrates / 0g Protein / 10mg Sodium / 10g Sugar

INGREDIENTS:

- 1 cup Limoncello
- 2 cups soda water or sparkling water
- 1/2 cup Prosecco (optional for extra fizz)
- Ice cubes (as needed)
- Lemon slices and fresh mint leaves (for garnish)

DIRECTIONS:

1. Fill each glass with ice cubes.
2. Pour 1/4 cup of Limoncello into each glass.
3. Add 1/2 cup of soda water or sparkling water to each glass.
4. If desired, top with a splash of Prosecco for an extra touch of bubbles.
5. Stir gently to combine.
6. Garnish with a lemon slice and a sprig of fresh mint for a refreshing finish.
7. Serve immediately and enjoy the light, citrusy taste.

TIP: For a sweeter twist, add a splash of simple syrup or a few fresh berries to the glass before mixing the spritz.

Cooking Measurements & Kitchen Conversions

Dry Measurements Conversion Chart

Teaspoons	Tablespoons	Cups
3 tsp	1 tbsp	1/16 c
6 tsp	2 tbsp	1/8 c
12 tsp	4 tbsp	1/4 c
24 tsp	8 tbsp	1/2 c
36 tsp	12 tbsp	3/4 c
48 tsp	16 tbsp	1 c

Liquid Measurements Conversion Chart

Fluid Ounces	Cups	Pints	Quarts	Gallons
8 fl.oz	1 c	1/2 pt	1/4 qt	1/16 gal
16 fl.oz	2 c	1 pt	1/2 qt	1/8 gal
32 fl.oz	4 c	2 pt	1 qt	1/4 gal
64 fl.oz	8 c	4 pt	2 qt	1/2 gal
128 fl.oz	16 c	8 pt	4 qt	1 gal

Liquid Measurements (Volume)

Standard	Metric
1/5 tsp	1 ml
1 tsp	5 ml
1 tbsp	15 ml
1 c (8 fl.oz)	240 ml
34 fl.oz	1 liter

Dry Measurements (Weight)

Standard	Metric
.035 oz	1 g
3.5 oz	100 g
17.7 oz (1.1 lb)	500 g
35 oz	1 kg

US to Metric Conversions

Standard	Metric
1/5 tsp	1 ml
1 tsp	5 ml
1 tbsp	15 ml
1 fl. oz	30 ml
1 c	237 ml
1 pt	473 ml
1 qt	.95 liter
1 gal	3.8 liters
1 oz	28 g
1 lb	454 g

Oven Temperatures Conversion

Fahrenheit	Celsius
250 °F	120 °C
320 °F	160 °C
350 °F	180 °C
375 °F	190 °C
400 °F	205 °C
425 °F	220 °C

1 Cup

1 cup = 8 fluid ounces

1 cup = 16 tablespoons

1 cup = 48 teaspoons

1 cup = 1/2 pint

1 cup = 1/4 quart

1 cup = 1/16 gallon

1 cup = 240 ml.

GRATITUDE

Dear Customer,

Thank you for choosing **"5-Ingredient Mediterranean Cookbook."** Your support means the world to me and my family. I'm truly grateful that you've welcomed this book into your kitchen. I hope these recipes inspire you to embrace the vibrant flavors, wholesome ingredients, and joyful spirit of Mediterranean cooking. Whether you're new to this lifestyle or looking to simplify your meal prep, I believe this book will help you create delicious, healthy meals that nourish both body and soul with minimal effort.

Cooking is more than just a daily task; it's an opportunity to connect with the people we love and the traditions we cherish. With this book, I hope to bring a bit of that warmth and connection into your home. I am honored that you've chosen to embark on this culinary journey with me, and I can't wait to hear about the memories you create around your table. Your trust in these recipes is a gift I don't take lightly, and I'm committed to making your cooking experience as enjoyable and rewarding as possible.

Thank you for being a part of this journey and for allowing me to be a part of yours.

With gratitude,

Myla Slobodian

Made in the USA
Las Vegas, NV
05 January 2025

15926444R00046